THE NOR Shaman

"According to Norse mythology, whoever drinks from the Mead of Poetry will gain the abilities of a scholar-poet and be able to solve any riddle or problem presented to them. With this beautifully written and powerfully instructive book, Evelyn Rysdyk has popped the cork on this precious elixir and is offering us a taste of the wisdom to be found in the teachings of northern European shamanism."

HILLARY S. WEBB, AUTHOR OF *EXPLORING SHAMANISM* AND *TRAVELING BETWEEN THE WORLDS: CONVERSATIONS WITH CONTEMPORARY SHAMANS*

"Wise woman Rysdyk opens the mysterious portals to the ancient ancestral female shamanic traditions of Scandinavia and invites us to connect with the spiritual power found therein. She is a knowledgeable, trustworthy, and generous guide."

MAMA DONNA HENES, URBAN SHAMAN AND AUTHOR OF *CELESTIALLY AUSPICIOUS OCCASIONS: SEASONS, CYCLES, AND CELEBRATIONS*

"*The Norse Shaman* skillfully weaves scholarly insight with an abundance of guided, hands-on experience. In an exceptionally clear and thorough voice, Evelyn Rysdyk inspires us to make the earth-honoring wisdom of the far north—and the magic of the distant past—come alive in our hearts, and in our world, today."

LLYN ROBERTS, COAUTHOR OF *SPEAKING WITH NATURE*, RECIPIENT OF THE NAUTILUS BOOK AWARDS GOLD MEDAL

"Evelyn Rysdyk uses her shaman's discerning heart and wide-ranging intelligence to unearth precious, hard-won wisdom from our northernmost European ancestors, integrating it with the latest findings in anthropology, genetics, and the unsettling lessons of quantum physics to offer us exciting new ways to understand our humanity and place in the Universe. This is a book to change your life. Do the exercises and you'll never feel alone and helpless again."

ELLEN WINNER, AUTHOR OF *WORLD SHAMAN* AND
THOUGHTS IN THE MIND OF GOD

"A fascinating journey through the history of European shamanism. Don't miss out on this captivating book!"

ROBBIE HOLZ, COAUTHOR OF *SECRETS OF ABORIGINAL HEALING*
AND *ABORIGINAL SECRETS OF AWAKENING*

"This book is a gem! Part historical review, part instruction manual, the author stokes the fires of her Norse heritage to warm the hearts and kindle the minds of her readers. Evelyn Rysdyk is a triple threat—a brilliant illustrator, a renowned shamanic healer and teacher, and a gifted writer at the height of her craft. A very satisfying read. Highly recommended."

PAUL BOWERSOX COAUTHOR OF *SEEING IN THE DARK*

"I love how this work blends the wisdom we find in mythology with the insights that modern technology, science, and new physics has given us. Evelyn is a shaman who embodies the knowledge and practice of Norse shamanism through ancestry, calling, profession, and daily life."

COLLEEN DEATSMAN, SHAMANIC PRACTITIONER, AUTHOR OF
THE HOLLOW BONE, AND COAUTHOR OF *SEEING IN THE DARK*

"Evelyn Rysdyk has written a very important book. For anyone longing to deepen their personal transformation, enhance their shamanic practice, help our modern society restore balance and harmony with nature and its inhabitants, and bring back the sacred feminine in all aspects of their lives, I recommend this book as an integral part of their toolbox."

CLAUDE PONCELET, PH.D., AUTHOR OF *THE SHAMAN WITHIN*

THE NORSE
Shaman

Ancient Spiritual Practices of
the Northern Tradition

Evelyn C. Rysdyk

Destiny Books
Rochester, Vermont • Toronto, Canada

Destiny Books
One Park Street
Rochester, Vermont 05767
www.DestinyBooks.com

Text stock is SFI certified

Destiny Books is a division of Inner Traditions International

Library of Congress Cataloging-in-Publication Data
Names: Rysdyk, Evelyn C., author.
Title: The Norse Shaman : ancient spiritual practices of the northern tradition /
    Evelyn C. Rysdyk.
Description: Rochester, Vermont : Destiny Books, 2016. | Includes bibliographical
    references and index.
Identifiers: LCCN 2016002898 (print) | LCCN 2016021724 (e-book) |
    ISBN 9781620555934 (pbk.) | ISBN 9781620555941 (e-book)
Subjects: LCSH: Shamanism--Europe, Northern.
Classification: LCC BF1622.E853 R97 2016 (print) | LCC BF1622.E853 (e-book) |
    DDC 293/.144—dc23
LC record available at https://lccn.loc.gov/2016002898

Printed and bound in the United States by Lake Book Manufacturing, Inc.
The text stock is SFI certified. The Sustainable Forestry Initiative® program
promotes sustainable forest management.

10   9   8   7   6   5   4   3   2   1

Text design and layout by Virginia Scott Bowman
This book was typeset in Garamond Premier Pro, Avenir, and Gill Sans with
Althelas, Hypatia Sans, and Garamond used as display typefaces

To send correspondence to the author of this book, mail a first-class letter to the
author c/o Inner Traditions • Bear & Company, One Park Street, Rochester, VT
05767, and we will forward the communication, or contact the author directly at
www.evelynrysdyk.com.

◎ ◎ ◎

This book is dedicated to my ancestors who, in spite of the inexplicable vagaries of evolution and unimaginable hardships of famine, hunger, war, and pestilence, managed to pass the sacred gift of physical existence to me. I honor and thank you deeply for making my life possible.

Author's Note

This book is not connected with the neo-pagan religion of Asatru, nor is it an attempt at accurately re-creating Viking Age traditions. Instead, it is an exploration of very ancient shamanic traditions that were preserved as fragments in Norse/Germanic myths and are part of our collective human history.

This book does not replace formal instruction in shamanic spirituality. The exercises in this book assume that you already know how to perform a shamanic journey. It is necessary that you know how to journey and have a strong connection to a power animal or teacher before you work with this book. If you haven't yet learned this process, I have provided an introduction to shamanic journeying in this book's first appendix. I also recommend that you read my book *Spirit Walking: A Course in Shamanic Power* to learn more about shamanic journeying and developing relationships with the helpful, healing spirits. Before you attempt any of the exercises in this book, read the instructions thoroughly, be sure that you understand them well, and be sure to gather all that you will require.

◎ ◎ ◎

The suggestions, processes, and shamanic techniques described in this book are in no way meant to replace professional medical or mental health assistance. This book is intended to be an informational guide and not to treat, diagnose, or prescribe. Always consult with a qualified health care professional regarding any medical or mental health condition or symptoms. Neither the author nor the publisher accepts any responsibility for your health or how you choose to use the information contained in this book.

Contents

Acknowledgments

I would like to honor my mother, Agnes M. (Blyseth) Rysdyk, who began her genealogical research before I was born—the lion's share of which was done many decades before computerized records and the Internet. (Many of my childhood car trips included visits to churches and graveyards!) Her curiosity and detective-like tenacity has given me the names and birthplaces for generations of my maternal and paternal ancestors going back several centuries.

On the home front, thanks to my wife and creative companion, Allie Knowlton—an extraordinary woman who enriches my life in ways beyond words. Thanks also to our cat Fylgja, who had to deal with me talking to myself and reading draft passages aloud during her naptime.

Several decades ago, the experiences I had in the West Kennet Long Barrow and so many other Neolithic sites in Britain awakened something very ancient and powerful that still echoes through my being. Thank you, Madeleine Burnside, for being my tour guide and brilliant co-conspirator back in those days.

Music is a great lubricant to my artistic flow, and each project seems to require a different playlist. This book needed the talents of Meg Bowles, Ian Brody, Bukkene Bruse, Frode Fjellheim, Agnes Buen Garnås, Hedningarna, Krauka, Pekka Lehti, Annbjørg Lien, Eivør Pálsdóttir, Ernst Reijseger, Graeme Revell, Robert Rich, Steve Roach,

Wimme Saari, Transjoik, Trio Mediaeval, Väsen, Wardruna, and of every brilliant performer on the *Wizard Women of the North* album.

Finally, I offer my deep gratitude to my incredible agent, Stephany Evans at FinePrint Literary Management and to Jon Graham at Inner Traditions for believing in this project.

Tusen Takk!

Simplified Pronunciation Guide to the Norse Words in This Book

Old Norse is no longer a living language. Scandinavian languages have some ties to Old Norse, but the language that retains the closest ties is Icelandic. As I am a native speaker of American English from an urban suburb of lower New York, I have done my best to provide you with a simplified guide to pronouncing the important words and names found in this book.

Old Norse and Scandinavian languages have a few unusual letters. The letters that are common with the English language are also pronounced somewhat differently. Below is a general guide to letter pronunciations that you will find in this book.

PRONUNCIATION OF OLD NORSE LETTERS

LETTER	EQUIVALENT	COMMENTS
a	g<u>o</u>t	
ä	<u>o</u>dd	
á	<u>o</u>dd	
å	st<u>o</u>re	Similar sound to ǫ (see below), but longer
b	<u>b</u>oat	
d	<u>d</u>eath	
ð	<u>th</u>en	Also like the th in weather. Capitalized "Eth" looks like this: Đ

PRONUNCIATION OF OLD NORSE LETTERS (cont'd)

LETTER	EQUIVALENT	COMMENTS
e	b_e_t	
g	English	But if the beginning of a word, doubled, or next to k, þ, s, or t, then like _g_o
h	_h_ouse	
i	_e_at	
j	_y_es	
k	_k_ick	
l	_l_ess	
m	_m_an	
n	_n_ever	
o	wr_o_te	A short, clipped sound
ö	b_i_rd/h_u_rt	
ø	b_i_rd/h_u_rt	
ǫ	st_o_rm	
p	_p_ill	
r	_r_oad	If you can manage a soft roll as in the Spanish word _rojo_, extra points!
s	_s_and	
t	_t_ime	
u	s_ou_p	
v	_v_ery	
ks	si_x_	
y	bl_ue_	
z	ra_ts_	
þ	_th_in	Also like the _th_ in _thunder_. Capitalized "Thorn" looks like this: Þ
æ	r_a_g	
au	h_ou_se	
ei	r_ai_n	
ey	b_oy_	

Now you're ready to try the list of words and names. Words have their emphasis on the first syllable. I recommend that you take a deep breath and remember to keep a lighthearted attitude while practicing the list. Be patient with yourself and realize you're probably going to make mistakes. Just do your best, and have fun with it!

PRONUNCIATION OF WORDS
COMMONLY FOUND IN THESE PAGES

NORSE WORD	PRONUNCIATION
Æsir	AH-sear
Bergsrå	BEARGS-row (Closer to the Norwegian pronunciation, which is a bit easier!)
Brisingamen	BREESING-ahmen
Freyja	FRAY-yah
fylgja	FEEL-yah
fylgjur	FEEL-yur
galdr	GAHL-dur
galdrakona	GAHL-DRA-kone-ah
gandreið	GON-drayth
hamskipti	HOM-skipf-tea
havsrå	HAVS-row
jötunn	YER-ton
landvættir	LOND-vaht-ear
Lif	LEAF
Lifthrasir	LEAF-thra-sear
Ljossalheim	YOH-SAL-heim
Mimir	MEEM-ear
Njörðr	NYER-thur
Óðinn	OHth-in (Swallow the th so it sounds more like Odin)
Ørlög	UR-leg (Closer to the Norwegian pronunciation, which is a bit easier!)

PRONUNCIATION OF WORDS
COMMONLY FOUND IN THESE PAGES (cont'd)

NORSE WORD	PRONUNCIATION
Ragnarök	RANGNAR-urk (Closer to the Norwegian pronunciation, which is a bit easier!)
Seiðhjallr	SAYTH-yolur
Seiðkona	SAYTH-kone-ah
Seiðman	SAYTH-mon
Seiðmaðr	SAYTH-manhr
Seiðr	SAYTH-ur
seiðstafr	SAYTH-staf-ur
sjörå	SHER-oh (Closer to the Norwegian pronunciation, which is a bit easier!)
skogsrå	SKOHGS-row (Closer to the Norwegian pronunciation, which is a bit easier!)
Skuld	SKOOLD
Sleipnir	SHLIPE-near
Urð	URth
Urðr	URthr (Closer to the Norwegian pronunciation, which is a bit easier!)
Urðarbrunnr	URTH-ah-broonr (Closer to the Norwegian pronunciation, which is a bit easier!)
Vanir	VON-ear
Vårdträd	VOAR-trod
Varðlok	VARth-lock
Varðlokur	VARth-lock-ur
Verðandi	VEARth-ahn-dee (Tongue forms the th, but stop short in pronouncing the sound)
Völ	VERL
Völur	VERL-ur
Völuspá	VERL-u-spoh

NORSE WORD	PRONUNCIATION
Wyrd	Vearhd (Like *weird* with a *v* sound)
Yggdrasil	EEG-dra-SIL (The last syllable is not as strong as the first)
Ymir	EE-mear
Þórbjörg lítilvölva	THOR-byerg LEETL-verl-vah

I have not provided any guidance for the pronunciations of the Sami words in this book. As I do not have a reliable source for any of the Sami languages, I chose not to make ill-informed recommendations in these pages. My apologies go to the people of Sápmi for the omission.

INTRODUCTION

The Power of Norse Shamanism

This book is an exploration of ancient shamanic traditions that were preserved as memories in the folk traditions of Northern Europe. I believe that archaeological discoveries and the ideas preserved in these mythic stories hold clues to the prehistoric shamanic ways of the ancestors. In addition, I believe that the tales of the Old Norse are metaphoric explanations of the profound discoveries that were made by these shamans of old. By examining evidence and through our own firsthand interactions with the spirits through sacred rituals, we have the opportunity to reconnect ourselves with humanity's rich spiritual history. This journey of reconnection will serve not only to heal our own hearts and reclaim the missing pieces of wisdom safeguarded by the ancestors but unite us again more deeply with the other beings in our larger planetary family.

For much of my adult life, I have immersed myself in the practice of shamanic spirituality. In the course of developing powerful connections with my tutelary spirits, my explorations led me to study core shamanism with Michael Harner, Ph.D., and Sandra Ingerman over twenty-five years ago. Broadening my studies, I have worked with indigenous shamans from Siberia, Central Asia, and the Andes mountains, and more extensively with a jhankri from the Himalayan region. Yet all that time, the voices of my blood ancestors called to me in my journeys.

Like many European Americans, my ancestors arrived on the shores of North America over a period of several hundred years. My father's English ancestors began to arrive here in the late seventeenth century. In the eighteenth century, his Dutch folk followed and gave our family their surname. The Germans and Scots who arrived in the nineteenth century added still more northern spice to my paternal line.

My mother's parents arrived here in the early twentieth century from Norway. My maternal grandmother was from a farming family living on the southern island of Tromøy and my grandfather from a fishing family living on the harsh and rugged coast in Bardal, which lies about halfway between Trondheim and the Lofoten Islands.

As a result of these ancestors' often perilous journeys across the Atlantic Ocean, I was born in the New World. Even though far from the place where they were born, those who preceded me preserved as much as they could of their ancestral traditions while learning the language and customs of their new home.

Being a firstborn, I had two sets of grandparents, great aunts and uncles, a great-grandmother and her siblings surrounding me. Blessedly, these elders were great storytellers. From the Norwegian spoken by my mother's family to the German-spiced stories my father's family told, strong elements of the old ways of Northern Europe were imprinted into my psyche. The stories of Europe's ancient trees, stone circles, rugged coasts, and deep fjords are woven into the fabric of my soul as certainly as the spirits who reside there.

Lodged just as deeply in my heart are feelings of sadness, revulsion, and horror at how many of my Northern European ancestors became brutal colonizers, waged two world wars, and exerted patriarchal dominance over other peoples and the environment. In my early life, it puzzled me how the same people that created extraordinary art, music, and literature could participate in creating so much damage in the world. As a shamanic healer, I have come to recognize that such behaviors have their basis in spiritual disconnection from nature and from the other beings who share our world. In a shamanic view, this disconnection results in a soul illness that creates deep feelings of weakness and inadequacy. Those feelings can create a desperate desire for power, which can lead to subjugating other people and other species and "claiming" vast tracts of land in the vain expectation of feeling whole. Tragically, the persistence of these destructive behaviors now jeopardizes the ultimate survival of our species and planet.

It is clear that somewhere between our earliest beginnings as hunter-gatherers who left Africa and the onset of these destructive behaviors, a very vital way of being was lost. This book is a path to recover the way our oldest ancestors once perceived themselves, nature, and the cosmos. It is important to resist the arrogant idea that myths of ancient people are, somehow, quaint stories filled with antiquated ideas of reality. Using the metaphoric information at the roots of ancient myths or stories and through experiential practices, we can discover a renewed sense of connection, respect, and personal power.

Let me explain a bit about the concept of *power*. The shaman or shamanic practitioner borrows power or enlivening spiritual energy from her spirit allies. These may include the animals, birds, landscape features, natural forces, energies from the elementals, and cosmic bodies and forces. In her work, the shaman may also borrow shamanic power or wisdom from human-form teachers and from her ancestors. These spiritual energies are invited to participate in the work of the shaman, who is always focused on mending connections and supporting harmony. Historically, the shaman, did not use her or his ego to direct the action of the spirits but worked alongside the spirits, and on behalf of the community, to provide healing, insight, divination, wisdom, and guidance for the purpose of enhancing the possibility for individual and group survival.

The Scandinavian languages of Danish, Norwegian, and Swedish have two words for power. They are *makt* and *kraft*.* *Kraft* refers to the power we think of as energy. For instance, a power plant that

---

*Many thanks to Jonathan Horwitz for sharing this marvelous linguistic insight.

produces energy is a *kraftverk* or energy works. When discussing the word in terms of shamanism, it refers to the energetic spiritual power that the shaman relies upon for his work. The other word, *makt*, refers to power as force or influence. This is used in the word *super-makt* or superpower, which refers to a dominant nation. This is power over something or someone and is the ego's idea of power. The true shaman or shamanic practitioner stays on the former side of power and continually works with his ego to avoid the pitfalls of falling into the latter.

Another point that I wish to stress is that while this book is focused on the shamanic threads woven through the region we now call Northern Europe, it is not meant to suggest that the practices covered in these pages are only for those who claim that heritage. Far more than we once realized, our archaic human ancestors roamed far and wide from their African homeland beginning well over 100,000 years ago. They populated the entirety of the Eurasia continent before subsequent waves of "modern" *Homo sapiens sapiens* arrived on the scene. When these newcomers met their archaic forebearers, they made connections and interbred. Current DNA research has shown beyond a shadow of doubt that not only are we all Africans at our core, every individual on the planet is a hybrid of modern and archaic human subspecies.[1] That stunning truth has tossed out the possibility that any of us might be a "purebred" person of any sort! There is only one human family tree, composed of many branches, which are each arrayed with a myriad of marvelous individuals. While we can feel a familial alliance to the branch into which we happen to have been born, any ideas we believe about racial or geo-political superiority are delusionary. Until every one of us and every living being is perceived as both sacred and precious, our future here will be uncertain. We need to lift all souls up and break down the barriers that interfere with our ability to work together. To save our-selves, we need to merge all the best of our ancestors' collective wis-dom with our own individual transformative capacities. This is our best chance for evolving our destructive trajectory to one of personal and planetary renewal.

Creating harmony and collaborating with the spirits of nature to support Life has always been the shaman's work. I hope this book will inspire you to manifest your unique part in Mother Nature's beautiful renaissance.

First Grandmother

You dreamed me into Life as you sang
Shaping grey mists of a time yet to be
You called me into being
Forming a feeling into flesh
You sang Life into me. Here.
A wandering child, Home again.

Shaper of bones and blood!
Dissatisfied with singular memories
You relinquished dusty anonymity
For Continuance.
A laughing Creatrix in her creation,
Breathing now in this body.

Working my sinew, scratching my skull
Incising whorls like fingerprints
Is this a code for me to break?
Or do they awaken songs
In this sacred bundle,
Uncovering what you secreted within.

I am eager to remember.

EVELYN RYSDYK

1
Visionaries in Our Family Tree

Observations of contemporary hunter-gatherer peoples reveal that they view the world from an animist perspective. Animism is the spiritual framework that understands that physical beings—including animals, plants, and even inanimate objects, landscape features, and phenomena—possess a spirit or animating essence. This cultural construct is intimately connected to the hunter-gatherer lifestyle. By viewing everything as alive, hunter-gatherers recognize that all of the elements of the landscape are coparticipants in the workings of life. Spirit is at the foundation of everything, and it is what makes all aspects of our physical existence possible. It is the framework on which physical existence is sustained.

Shamanism is a widely practiced spiritual tradition. While the forms this tradition takes are many, the root of the tradition is the practice of negotiating harmony with the spirits by fostering relationships with them. The shaman knows that we are surrounded by sentient beings who can offer their wisdom, guidance, perspectives, and healing power in support of human life. In return for these gifts, the people offer their respect and nurturance to the spirits. This mutually respectful and honorific interaction is the basis for shamanic culture.

We can suppose that since our most ancient ancestors lived a hunting and gathering existence, they also had similar spiritual worldviews to these contemporary hunter-gatherer groups; that is, that they practiced some form of shamanism.[1]

A shaman is someone who intentionally traverses the boundary of physical reality. This is done to better interact with the numinous beings that enliven nature. While spirits are nearly impossible to see or hear with our ordinary senses, the shaman is able to interact with these beings easily by moving beyond their ordinary way of perceiving the world. The shaman enters the realm of the spirits by expanding consciousness. This intentional journey between the ordinary and nonordinary realms is what defines a shaman and is the source of her or his strength, power, and ability to solve community problems. The shaman's altered state of consciousness—or trance—may be induced through several time-honored methods. These can include sensory or physical deprivation, meditation, or by the use of repetitive sensory stimuli such as intensive, prolonged dancing, rattling, chanting, flickering lights, or drumming.

Indeed, trance states and shamanism are intimately connected. James L. Pearson does an excellent job of connecting these dots in his book *Shamanism and the Ancient Mind* when he writes about the etymology of the words *trance* and *shaman*. He wrote that the word *trance* derives from the Latin *transitus*, "a passage," and that the verb root is *transive*, meaning "to pass over." Following this logic, he suggests that the word *trance* refers to entering another world. He further added that the term *shaman*, from the Tungus-Mongol word *šaman*, is both a noun and a verb. The Indo-European root *ša-* means both "to know" and "one who is excited, moved, raised." Through these linguistic explorations, Pearson determined that a shaman is, by definition, one who attains an ecstatic state and, furthermore, that entering a trance state is a prerequisite for shamanism.[2]

Michael Winkleman suggests that shamanism is endemic to nomadic hunting and gathering cultures. Indeed, evidence in the form of both portable objects and paintings on cave walls does support the idea that shamanism was prevalent across Europe during this time period. The abstract patterns from Upper Paleolithic cave walls—such as dots, wavy lines, spirals, and concentric circles—are consistent with entopic imagery* or visions that one sees during the early stages of a trance state.[3] In his book *Shamanism and the Ancient Mind,* James L. Pearson also agrees that the universal neurological and psychological experiences that result from altered-states experiences help to explain art that was created to either literally portray or suggest the shamanic trance state.

Apparently we are wired for altered-consciousness experiences. A study published in 1973 found that altered states of consciousness are virtually universal in their distribution across human societies. The study sampled 488 societies and found that fully 90 percent of those sampled groups exhibit institutionalized, culturally patterned forms of altered states of consciousness. The study also concluded that the capacity to experience an altered state of consciousness was so universal that it seems to be part of the psychobiological heritage of our species.[4]

Mike Williams, Ph.D., in his book *Prehistoric Belief,* is even more straightforward in his clarity about our ancestors' spiritual worldview, suggesting that people in prehistory were very adept at entering trance. During these trance states they would befriend the spiritual entities they met and treated those beings and the realms that they inhabited as another aspect of life.[5] In other words, our ancestors were comfortable with the understanding that there were otherworldly beings and realms beyond our own.

It is his belief that experiencing trance states was not an activity that was only limited to shamans. You see, our *Homo sapiens sapiens*† ancestors had fully modern brains. As such they were capable of a "higher order

---

*Visual experiences arising from anywhere within the optic system, which includes the eyes, the occipital lobe of the brain, and the many other portions of the neural cortex that process visual stimuli.

†Research that has come to light after Williams's book is suggesting that our *Homo sapiens neanderthalensis* and *Homo sapiens denisova* may have also had similar "modern" brain structures.

consciousness," which is the ability to conceive ideas of past, present, and future, of the dreaming and waking states, and of altering consciousness. Like us, these people also were capable of holding on to the memories of dream and altered-consciousness experiences. As a result, this higher order consciousness allows us to remember and relate different experiences of consciousness to our everyday existence. Directly because we humans have this ability, ideas that are born in dreams and visionary states can be used to inform and transform everyday reality.

Fire was critical to life in the north. A central fire was a pivot point around which life revolved once the sun's rays vanished into evening. Our ancestors spent their nights clustered around it to draw warmth, light, and comfort from its marvelous flickering. In our contemporary world, it is difficult to imagine the extraordinary darkness of an ancient night. We are so used to artificially illuminating our world. For us, day and night have become blended into each other. It is only in places far from civilization that it is still possible to get a taste of the true darkness. I had such an experience in the hours before dawn while hunting in upstate New York. It was a night without a moon, and the sky was so full of stars that it was impossible to discern any familiar constellations. In that darkness the old expression of not being able to see your hand in front of your face suddenly became a reality. The darkness was so complete that it was both physically disorienting and emotionally unsettling.

How comforting a fire is in such a circumstance! A fire creates a space where we can see and interact with each other. The small illuminated region around the fire becomes our whole world. The edges of the firelight also create a visual boundary. The space that lies beyond the firelight seems even darker. When gazing out to that darkness, our known world seems completely enfolded by another place.

When you sit in front of a fire in that deep darkness, the objects and people around you seem to shimmer and move in the flickering light. Firelight produces a stroboscopic effect where darkness and light alternate rapidly back and forth. The rhythmic rate at which this occurs

Fig. 1.1 Everywhere our species settled during the Paleolithic we created handprints. The making of these imprints spanned many generations. Perhaps it was important to our ancestors to communicate through images, "I was here. Now, you join me."

approximates low alpha- and theta-wave brain states. This brain activity is consistent with the experience of the shamanic state of consciousness.[6] Since life revolved around the fire, our ancestors were exposed to the trance-inducing, photic driving of firelight every evening of their lives. Altered consciousness is not only natural to our species, we have been doing it for hundreds of thousands of years.

This state assists in creating new connections between neurons. In other words, trance assists in "rewiring" the brain. If this is true, it is not so much that shamanism is a part of our ancient way of relating to the world around us, it is what helped us to understand ourselves (self-awareness) and our relationship with the world, enabled us to remember the past, and ponder our future. In other worlds, trance contributed in creating us as a species.[7] In addition, there are physiological and psychological benefits that occur when individuals enter trance that have been observed by scientists, not the least of which includes a better immune response.[8]

Trance is also an excellent problem-solving tool. Indeed, this is so clear that anthropologist Michael Harner suggests that voluntary entrance into a shamanic trance (shamanic state of consciousness) in a counseling context is a proven concrete problem-solving method.* Certainly, most people have experienced the spontaneous shift of consciousness that accompanies a "mindless" repetitive task such as spinning wool or listening to a repetitive sound. While this can be disconcerting when it happens unbidden, it can also be very beneficial. When I was a young illustrator, I frequently rode an old diesel commuter train into New York City. Morning and evening, the clickity-clack of the train would lull me into a dreamy trance. During these experiences I would often receive sudden insight about a current challenge. This method became so useful to me that I learned to use my hours on the train to help me solve creative problems, especially when I was on a tight deadline.

Being able to voluntarily enter a trance state would have been an invaluable tool for locating game for a community that relied upon seasonal arrivals of migrating animals, birds, and fish. The same would have been true in locating a lost member of the group, finding the reasons for illness, or discovering the right plant remedy to cure it. Indeed, finding any critical information that was hidden from ordinary sight, hearing, or touch could have meant the difference between perishing and surviving for our hunter-gatherer ancestors.

---

*More on Michael Harner and Harner Shamanic Counseling can be found at www.shamanism.org.

TECHNICIANS OF ECSTASY

During the days of our earliest ancestors, every individual in the community was required to participate in the survival of the group. People of all ages and of both sexes gathered plants and bird eggs, fished, picked berries, made tools, created shelters, and gathered firewood to sustain the tribal group.[9] Of course, as is the case today, there would have been individuals within the group who were better at certain tasks. Some people would have been more skilled at stalking game, making cordage, kindling a fire, or other tasks and so would have become "specialists" in their communities. This specialization would have been efficacious for the community, as those with better skills could accomplish essential tasks more rapidly and more consistently. This would have made group survival more certain. Even as we made our cultural transition from hunting and gathering into subsistence agricultural and pastoral lifestyles, skill specialization would have been beneficial for a group's survival success.

While entering trance state is a common human ability, as with any other human skill, some individuals are more able to achieve a trance state than others. Indeed, it is most likely that there is a genetic component affecting a person's ability to more easily enter the shamanic state of consciousness.[10] Just as the more nimble-fingered people would have been better at knapping flint, weaving fishing nets, and setting snares, the people either psychologically or physiologically predisposed to enter trance states at will would have become the community shamans.

In experiencing trance states with regularity, our ancestors would have experienced a blurring of what we would delineate as natural and supernatural realities. In other words, their environment would have contained both physical and spiritual beings. In the same way that all physical aspects of the environment were viewed as participants in daily survival, these spiritual beings would have certainly been perceived in a similar light. Since these beings were not usually visible in this plane of existence, the shaman's skill of willfully entering trance would have been essential for communication with them. For this reason, the shaman would have been an invaluable member of a community.

SHAMANIC WORLDVIEW

Shamanic cultures recognize that we are so interconnected that we are in a constant dance of mutual impact upon one another. Since shamanism is a historical and global phenomenon, this worldview is most certainly a part of our collective human history.

There are also many similarities from one shamanic culture to the next. It certainly stands to reason that some of these ideas common to all shamanic cultures arose in our earliest hunter-gatherer past. For instance, shamanic cultural ideology commonly includes the following elements.

Everything Has a Spirit

In the animist hunter-gatherer worldview, our surrounding environment is inhabited by spiritual entities. These supernatural beings have the power for both good and unbeneficial action. The power and influence of these beings may vary widely from highly constructive to detrimentally negative.

The shaman can interact with spirit beings of many different shapes. These spirits may have a humanlike form (anthropomorphic) or animal-like form (zoomorphic) or may shape-shift between the two or have both human and animal elements (therianthropic). Indeed, some beings may also share attributes with the plant world (phytomorphic) or have forms that are blended with landscape features such as stones.

Spirits Have a Dynamic and Multifaceted Nature

While the spirit is what animates and enlivens all beings, spirits are also capable of leaving the physical form either completely or partially. When done intentionally by a shaman, this "spirit flight" can provide access to the spirits. However, this is always done with great caution.

Even partial spirit loss may cause illness just as a complete loss of the spirit results in death. For this reason a shaman fully masters the art of spirit travel, monitors the length of the journey, and always takes a trusted spirit protector/companion along on the experience. A shaman may also use talismans or ritual protection to protect the physical body while in an altered state.

Wandering spirits can also populate the realm of the living. Souls of deceased beings may continue to roam after the death of their host body. In the case of game animals, these spirits are fed and placated so that they return again to physical form. The spirits of deceased people must also be cared for so that they do not disturb the living.

The Shaman's Journey and the Realms of Spirit

The shamanic journey* is a way to expand perception beyond one's ordinary senses. In this expanded state of awareness, it is possible to communicate with the spiritual world and receive information, guidance, insight, or healing to support physical reality. The shaman would be called upon to locate hidden sources of food, find a remedy to aid the sick, or communicate with the ancestors. It is even thought that shamanic trance states may have guided our ancestors' steps as they embarked on their epic journeys out of the places of Africa.[11]

The spirit world is not bound by the same rules of time and space that define the physical world. As a result, a bridge is necessary so that our minds can understand the information we receive from that plane. Since this process originated with our hunter-gatherer ancestors, the structure of the journey process parallels their way of relating to the world. Each day, a hunter-gatherer group begins by departing their sleeping place and central fire to travel through the landscape. On that physical journey, they accumulate food, shelter materials, water, and

---

*A basic introduction to shamanic journeying can be found in this book's appendices. A more detailed description of the shamanic journey process can be found in my book *Spirit Walking: A Course in Shamanic Power*, or in Sandra Ingerman's book *The Beginner's Guide to Shamanic Journeying*.

other things necessary to sustain their survival. At the close of day, the group gathers together by the fire again to share the bounty found on their travels.

A shamanic journey into the realms of spirit has a similar framework and would have been used to "gather" what was needed for survival but was unable to be perceived with ordinary senses. A shaman begins her or his journey in a starting place and then alters consciousness to "travel" through the spiritual landscape. Once the shaman receives what information is necessary, she or he returns to ordinary consciousness.

To alter consciousness, a shaman may use many different methods to achieve trance or what is known as the shamanic state of consciousness (SSC). These may include intentional deprivation (fasting or sleeplessness), using psychoactive substances,* and by the use of repetitive stimuli such as flickering lights or monotonous sounds such as drumming.

Geography of the Spirit World

Shamanic cosmology describes a spiritual world with multiple levels. The Upper World, Middle World, and Lower World are realms in which the spirits reside. Our physical existence is a part of the Middle World. Multiple upper and lower worlds may exist for a shaman depending upon her individual culture or spiritual training. The realms are united by the central axis, which is commonly represented as a great tree, pillar, pole, or mountain. This axis mundi provides a way for the shaman to enter the upper and lower worlds as well as return safely to the human realm.

During these journeys, the shaman interacts with the spirit world and the beings that reside there to provide solutions to problems in the human world. Attention is paid to keeping relationships between humans, the natural world, and the spirits in balance. A shaman may

---

*Along with plants such as *ayahuasca* and San Pedro or peyote cactuses, our ancestors may have ingested certain animal brains for the same purpose. An article on this topic, "Venuses, Turtles and Other Hand-held Cosmic Models," was written by Bethe Hagens and published in 1991.

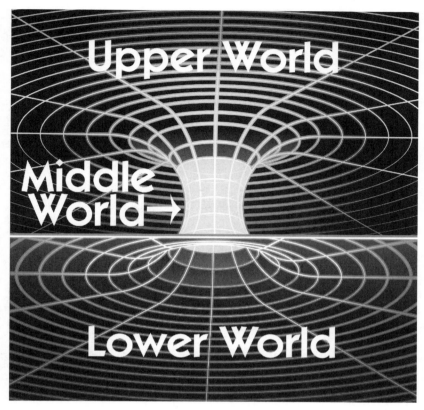

Figure 1.2. The idea that multiple realms of the spirit exist is common to most shamanic cultures. Some cultures further subdivide these three realms into even more.

journey to one world or to many in the course of his journey; however, it is the shaman's return that is the most important aspect of his spirit flight. The shaman travels to better this world by negotiating with spirits, creating harmony, or finding information that is critical to supporting life. If the shaman doesn't return, the purpose of the journey is forfeited.

Reciprocity with Nature and the Spirit World

Since all of nature is alive and is necessary for human survival, it is important to maintain harmonious relationships with the "other" beings that inhabit it. Some form of communication is necessary for facilitating and maintaining a mutually constructive relationship. In the same way we keep our "balance sheet" of giving and taking equitable with our human companions, maintaining good relationships with the Earth and her animals, birds, and plants requires similar attention. Since nature directly provides everything needed for the people to survive, hunter-gatherers make offerings to the spirits in the natural world to balance all that we are given. These offerings can be to landscape features such as sources of freshwater, to game animals' ancestors (master spirits) so that they continue to repopulate the physical world with bounty for hunters, to human ancestors, or indeed to any other spirits who might have influence over human existence.

A shaman's role in any society is to act as a facilitator between the human realm and that of the other beings and spirits that inhabit the environment. Through interaction with them, our shaman ancestors came to understand that our intrinsic interdependencies sustain life. In a shamanic culture, individuals value harmony with their environment, as they have an intimate understanding of their dependence on it. There is a value placed on cooperation and cohesiveness rather than mastery of and control over the environment, as there tends to be a deeper sense of the value of all aspects of life.[12]

I refer to this shamanic perspective of respectful interplay as Reverent Participatory Relationship.[13] This idea suggests that all interactions—whether with other humans, with the creatures of the physical landscape, or with supernatural beings—be undertaken in an atmosphere of consideration and honor. To encourage harmony it is necessary to be attentive, to maintain mutual connection, and to care well for each other.

Sharing Power

The many spirit beings that inhabit the world are also potential sources of power for the shaman. The power-filled relationships forged with the spirits give the shaman abilities to perform services to the community such as healing and divination that would otherwise be beyond the reach of ordinary human capabilities. Through nurturing relationships, a shaman is able to "borrow" power from other beings to better accomplish her tasks. In the same way that we have human companions who may be called upon when we need help, shamans might borrow the strength of a bear, the sight of an eagle, or the healing power of a plant to assist them in their work. Relationships with the spirits are nurtured through repeated communication, through respectful action, and by nurturance through ceremony or by making offerings.

Harmony and Ritual

The visible and invisible aspects of the environment provide all that is necessary for life. This means that we are already in relationship with the game animals, the rivers, the air, the plants, and the weather. Since we are continually being provided with many benefits, rituals of communication, of thanksgiving, and of gift giving become necessary in order to facilitate balance.

Even a brief examination of shamanic cultures around the world reveals that every one has developed a system of ritual reciprocity for maintaining harmony with the spirits.

Ritual Spaces

The metaphoric and symbolic landscape of a shaman's journey can become imprinted on ordinary landscape, blurring delineations between ordinary and supernatural worlds. In this way a certain outcropping of stone may become an entrance into the spirit world, an ancient tree can stand in for the World Tree, an animal den may be the home of a species' "master spirit" and so forth. This is true of many indigenous hunter-gatherer or substance agricultural and pastoralist peoples who practice shamanism. Living close to nature allows you to more easily perceive that the numinous is always within reach.

Repeated rituals in a location can also imbue a place with powerful spiritual significance. In either case, an imprint of the spiritual geography overlays the ordinary landscape.[14]

Navigating this shamanic geography suggests that:

- All areas may be ritual spaces as need arises.
- Some areas may be dedicated specifically for ritual only and are thought of as especially sacred. Activities in these specialized areas involve doorways for communication and gift giving with the supernatural world.
- These locations can be for maintaining relationship and honoring of household, ancestral, cosmological, legendary, or ceremonial spirits and events.
- Burial or cremation sites may be ritual sites to commune with the dead.
- Activities in any of these sacred spaces involve creation or deposition of physical gifts within the symbolic context of maintaining balanced relationship.

◈ *Engaging with Fire*

While it is impossible to roll back the ages to live exactly in the manner of our shamanic predecessors we can do some things to help us better understand their spiritual landscape. We do this by intentionally setting up similar experiences. This provides the opportunity to more fully embody a deeper understanding of their way of knowing the world. Since our ancestors are a part of us, the ancient memories of the spirits held within us can awaken.

Before you proceed with the exercise, please read through it thoroughly and gather all that you need. If you are unsure about some of the aspects of the exercise below, please read my book *Spirit Walking: A Guide to Shamanic Power.*

For this exercise, you will need:

- Either a safe outdoor fire ring or indoor fireplace
- Tinder, kindling, and firewood for a sacred fire
- Matches or other ignition source

Figure 1.3. Fire is one very effective way our ancestors
used to alter their consciousness.

- Your rattle or drum
- Cornmeal
- An aromatic offering of evergreen needles
- Your journal or a notebook and pen
- A way to extinguish the fire in an emergency

◈ Making the Journey

1. Choose a time when you will be able to spend a few hours with the fire
   until it goes completely out.

2. Prepare yourself by cleansing yourself and the location where the fire is to be prepared as you might for a special time with a treasured loved one. Once physically clean, honor the spirits of all directions and ask them to bless the area where you will be working. You may also use an aromatic substance to "sweeten" the air of the area, such as the smoke from incense or evergreen needles.

3. Then gather all your preparatory materials, such as your drum and rattle, your other sacred tools, and all the firewood and kindling you will need. Do this in a prayerful manner with the purpose of the ceremony held in your heart. Keep safety in mind at all times as you are working, and if you are going to build a fire outdoors, have a bucket of water on hand to quench any errant sparks.

4. Make an offering in the fireplace or on the ground in the fire ring that will receive the fire. Thank the place for holding the fire for you. I use fir needles, cornmeal, honey, or alcohol for this purpose. However, you may use whatever you normally use for an offering.

5. Now set up a small fire, but do not light it yet. Once the kindling and firewood are ready to receive the match, begin rattling softly. Call your power animal and teacher to you, and begin to hum or tone from your heart. (If you know your shamanic power song this is an excellent time to sing it.*)

6. Let the fire know that you want to learn to see as your ancestors once did. Then light the fire. As the wood begins to catch, sing more loudly with the intent of honoring the fire spirit with your song. To show gratitude to the fire spirit for working with you, toss a small bit of offering material into the flames to feed it.

7. When the fire is full, sit as close to it as you can safely, and gaze deeply into the fire. Allow the fire spirit to teach you. You may see images in the flames or you may hear voices whispering to you. The spirits will communicate with your heart in their own way. As the fire dies to coals,

---

*See the author's book *Spirit Walking: A Course in Shamanic Power,* pages 85–88, to determine your shamanic power song.

it will continue to provide information and connection, so it is important to stay with the fire until it goes out completely. As the embers cool, you may journal what you have received.

8. When through, make another offering to your helping spirits and to the fire for their loving assistance.

On the next morning when you are sure the last of the coals are completely cold, take a bit of the ashes and mix them with cornmeal or flour to sprinkle on the earth. Again thank the ancestors, the fire, the air, the wood, and earth for their gifts.

You may have a very clear idea of what you learned or may have to sit with the experience for a while to understand what you were given. Allow your heart to receive the gifts.

◈ Journey Explorations

- Journey to a teacher or power animal to ask, "What is the most important thing I gained from being with the fire spirit?" Record the content of your journey and your perceptions about what you received.

- Journey to a teacher or power animal to ask, "How can I use fire to see the spirit realms?"

After each journey, thank your helping spirits, and make an offering outdoors.

◈ Process Questions

- Write down in your journal what it was like to be with the fire.

- What did you learn about using the fire to "see" the spirit world? Write down all that you felt.

- How does it feel to have begun connecting with an ancestral way of knowing? Record your impressions.

2

Long Ago and Far Away

Discovering Our Ancestors' Gifts

Shamans believe that we are one with everything. This deep kinship with other beings allows us to assume one another's shape and garner one another's wisdom. By so doing, we come away with a different perspective. The illusionary barriers of the Western cultural paradigm, which separate us from the natural world, fall away so that we are once again relating to the world in the way of our shamanic ancestors.

I was recently asked why I believe that working with ancestral energies is so important. My answer is because they directly affect how we live our lives. While our ancestors may no longer be alive in their own bodies, they continue to exist in ours. In every one of our cells, we carry a sacred bundle of many thousand generations worth of genetic material that was given to us by our ancestors. Not only are they alive in our bodies, their spirits are able to assist us with our daily lives.

A series of studies done in 2010, published in the *European Journal of Social Psychology*, compared those who thought about their ancestors with those who made no preparation before taking a series of problem-solving and intelligence tests intended to measure how effective an individual is at meeting the challenges that may arise in everyday life.[1]

The results of the tests proved beyond a shadow of doubt that people who considered their ancestors before taking the tests received significantly higher scores. Reconnection with the ancestral energies imbued participants with better intellectual performance and enhanced their ability to find solutions. In other words, connecting with our forebearers—even through memory and imagination—enhances our ability to accomplish the challenges of life with more ease and confidence. Interestingly, the tests provided the same results whether or not the test subjects knew or even liked their ancestors! In every situation, simply thinking about their ancestors provided the participants with a clear advantage. It is now possible for us to see that the "primitive" tribal cultures across our planet that venerate their ancestors have had the right idea all along. Simply by keeping our ancestors close at heart and in our minds, we are far more able to solve the emotional, mental, and physical puzzles that life presents us, with measurably more skill and grace.

Thanks to my mother, who has devoted over six decades of her life to unraveling the details of her and her husband's heritage, I know the names, birthplaces, and ages of my ancestors all the way back to the early sixteenth century on both sides of my family. In an effort to go even further into the deep ancestry of her line, my mother sent her genetic material to National Geographic Society's Genographic Project when it was launched in 2005.[2] There, the scientists isolated my mother's mitochondrial DNA (mtDNA). Different from the mixed nucleic DNA we get from both our mother and father, mtDNA is passed unchanged from mother to daughter* through the generations. The only way that this aspect of our genetic material is altered is through the effects of subtle mutations that occur spontaneously over time. Because mitochondrial DNA is transmitted from mother to child (both male and female) as an intact package, it can be a useful tool in genealogical research into a person's maternal line. In other words, it is possible to trace a family line back from daughters to mothers and grandmothers until the first

---

*Men also receive mitochondrial DNA (mtDNA) from their mothers but cannot pass it to the next generation. The Y chromosome is passed as an intact package of genetic information from father to son and therefore may be used in a similar fashion as mtDNA to trace the male genetic line.

woman who carried the same copy of the genetic variation is discovered. Not only is this a way to better understand ourselves, it is a way to feel more personally connected to all of our relations in the deep past. I say "all of our relations" because not only are all human beings a part of the same family that arose in southeastern Africa, we are also a part of the living fabric of all creatures on the Earth.

The common direct maternal ancestor of every human being alive today was born in Africa around 180,000 years ago. Although she was not the only woman alive at the time, her mitochondrial genetic line is the only one that survived into the present. A small band of her descendants left their home in Africa and headed north around 100,000 years ago. In Africa and along the way in our planetwide journey, we met archaic humans and exchanged nucleic DNA. Thanks to archaic humans such as *Homo erectus, Homo sapiens neanderthalensis,* and *Homo sapiens denisova,* modern humans acquired subtle mutations and adaptations that gave our ancestors enriched immunity, allowed them to eat a wider variety of food, and so gave us the ability to follow new horizons.[3] Approximately 60,000 to 70,000 years ago, some of these wanderers had made it to the area we now refer to as the Middle East.

It bears mentioning here that the places we have named Europe, the Middle East, and Asia are actually part of one enormous landmass—Eurasia. This megacontinent stretches from the western coasts of Ireland and Portugal to Kamchatka in the east, across the far north Arctic regions of Scandinavia to the Bering Sea and southward to the tropical tip of the Indian subcontinent.

DNA compared from ancient samples and contemporary findings from the Genographic Project suggest that modern humans migrated into western Eurasia in several separate waves.[4] These migrations began during the Upper Paleolithic* period, which began around 50,000 years ago. During this time frame, our ancestors arrived in the western part of Eurasia we refer to as Europe somewhere between 45,000 and

---

*The year ranges of these epoch designations vary from area to area as they refer to technological and cultural changes more than being simple time scales.

Figure 2.1. This figure, now known in academic circles as the
"Woman of Willendorf," is a 4.4-inch-tall Paleolithic
limestone carving, which had been originally covered in red ochre.
It was unearthed in Lower Austria in 1908.

43,000 years ago. These so-called Cro-Magnon people painted cave walls, made flutes, created jewelry, and produced portable sculptures of humans, animals, and hybridized animal/human figures of ivory, bone, ceramic, and stone.[5] Over a period of two to three thousand years, humans settled all the way from what is now known as Italy to southern England.[6]

Over the passage of time, mitochondrial DNA sustains subtle mutations. Each subsequent mutation produces a variation on the genetic theme that our mitochondrial Eve carried. These variations are called haplogroups and allow us to track the paths of each branch of our human family tree as we spread across the Earth.

The most common mutation of mitochondrial DNA found in today's western European population (H haplogroup)* arose about 28,000 years ago. Around 20,000 to 26,000 years ago early Europeans retreated to southern areas, as living conditions had become far colder and drier during the period known as the Last Glacial Maximum. During this severe climatic period, the population shrank drastically, reducing the number of people in Europe. Beginning around 15,000 years ago, the great ice sheets began to retreat, and humans began moving northward again. The mitochondrial DNA lineage represented most often in the group that traveled north during this time was also part of the H haplogroup. For this reason, H mtDNA haplogroup variants remain the most common in European Eurasia today.

Whether my mitochondrial DNA ancestor was among the early settlers or a part of the second, postglacial migration may never be known. However, by approximately 14,000 years ago, my genetic ancestors were living in what is now northern Britain and southern Scandinavia just before the brief colder period referred to by science as the Younger Dryas, when the ice sheets made a temporary return.†

It is clear that the people who lived in this region—indeed, anywhere during the Upper Paleolithic and Mesolithic ages—had to have been incredibly resilient and resourceful. In appearance and ability, they looked the same and were as intelligent as modern people. Looking deeper into what we know about their lifestyle may give us clues to what they believed about the world and their ideas of spirit, which may lead us closer to our communal shamanic connections.

In studying the composition of their bones, we know that they

---

*My mitochondrial DNA is a part of this haplogroup. Along with all my *Homo sapiens sapiens* ancestors, I also carry DNA of two other subspecies hominid groups. Of my mtDNA, 2.9 percent is *Homo sapiens neanderthalensis* DNA and 0.7 percent is genetic material passed to me by my *Homo sapiens denisova* ancestors.

†This occurred very rapidly, in as few as ten years due to a significant reduction of the North Atlantic thermohaline circulation. This circulation of warm water into Europe from what we now call the Gulf Stream would have been halted by the catastrophic release of freshwater from enormous glacial lakes. This in turn would have prevented warm weather from reaching Europe.

made use of the ocean's resources such as fish, marine mammals, sea vegetables, and shellfish. They also hunted reindeer, moose, deer, wolverines, and beaver across the taiga forests and tundra; harvested plants, nuts, and berries; and fished the many rivers that traversed the postglacial landscape. Archaeological evidence suggests that inhabitants of the last Ice Age communities were flexible opportunists that made use of all available survival resources.[7] In other words, as all of our ancestors before them, these late Upper Paleolithic and Mesolithic Eurasians were hunters and gatherers.

Sea levels were up to 200 feet lower* than today. As a result, much more coastal land was available for habitation. For instance, the European mainland was connected to what is now Britain and southern Scandinavia by roughly 29,000 square miles (75,110 square kilometers) of dry land. Now submerged, this territory, referred to as Doggerland, was fertile hunting and gathering territory of rolling plains cut through by rivers, streams, lakes, and marshland that bordered the sea. The confluence of resources from the ocean, freshwater, fields, and forests provided an enormous bounty for the people who roamed Northern Europe.

Doggerland's lowland area allowed the people to travel after spending winter in what is now France and Britain to the midcoast of Norway for the summer months. This allowed our ancestors to follow migrating game and the geographic progression of ripening plants. Like the nomadic hunter-gatherers of northern Siberia who were observed by late nineteenth-century ethnographers such as Maria Czaplicka, these late Ice Age people lived in temporary camps during their travels, as well as in semipermanent dwellings that were repeatedly used at either end of their migration routes.[8]

The ancestors' survival strategy of hunting and gathering all across these rich lands allowed them to flourish. This lifestyle was so successful that it persisted for a long time in European Eurasia even during severe climate shifts. During this period, the climate underwent

---

*For comparison, this is the height of a typical fifteen- to eighteen-story office building. At the peak of the Ice Age, sea levels were as much as 400 feet lower than at present.

several drastic changes that influenced the plants, animals, and water levels. These changes had a huge impact on the lives of people living all over the inhabited world. As the climate swung from warmer to icy and back again, the migration routes of animals and plant species available for food changed dramatically. During these radical and sudden changes in temperature, entire regions flipped from forests to tundra and back again. Some of these climatic shifts occurred within the very short time periods ranging from an impossibly brief ten years to just a few generations.[9] As a result, our ancestors had to adapt their hunting and gathering methods to suit the shifting food sources. They must have faced times of severe famine. Yet the survivors also became so skilled at survival that the Neolithic agricultural evolution did not occur in the region of far Northern Europe until approximately 4,000 to 5,000 years ago. That is about fifteen centuries later than in other areas on the continent. Evidence suggests that the high density of hunter-gatherers in Northern Europe limited the northward dispersal of farming culture.[10]

Elders in these hunter-gatherer groups would have held the environmental knowledge necessary for survival. In an oral culture, the elderly function as a living library—a repository of all the collected methods and wisdom a tribe has gathered. Their lifelong observations of migrating birds and animals would have provided key information about when to travel to take advantage of seasonal resources. Shamans too would have been vital in determining when and where to travel, particularly during this period of intense climatic shifts. For instance, during the Mesolithic period, the land was being radically reshaped by the rising water levels fueled by melting glaciers. The most rapid rises of sea level were on the order of 3 to 6 feet a century, but because of the variable topography of the land, the flooding would not have been even.[11]

Around 8,200 years ago a series of events challenged the survival of these people even more dramatically. After nearly a millennia of incremental sea level rises, an enormous glacial lake the size of an inland sea, called Lake Agassiz, suddenly released an enormous amount of

Figure 2.2. Just as a stone picked up by a beachcomber is forever displaced from its original home, the people of Northern Europe were displaced over 8,200 years ago by forces beyond their control.

freshwater. This release immediately raised global sea levels an additional 2 feet and drowned much of the remaining territory of low-lying Doggerland. As a final insult, a huge underwater landslide off the coast of Norway created a tsunami that inundated the remaining coastline. The tsunami caused by the Storegga Slide also cut the ocean channel that separated Britain from Europe.

During this period, the landscape of European Eurasia would have been irrevocably transformed. Reliable hunting grounds and fishing areas would have vanished. Cut off from ancestral hunting, fishing, and burial grounds, the people living there would have felt a profound sense of being uprooted, ungrounded, and spiritually adrift.[12] In addition, the catastrophic floods most certainly involved large-scale loss of life in a population that was already very sparse. These losses would have invariably hit vulnerable members of the population such as children and elders much harder. While a loss of children is a horrific tragedy, having fewer wisdom-carrying elders could have had a tremendous impact on survivors of the devastating event. When elders die suddenly, the vital information stored in their memories is lost with them. Such a loss could have jeopardized the survival of the entire group. As a result, any elders who survived a catastrophe would have been incredibly precious and vital to the success of those who remained.

Around this same time period, a new wave of immigration had begun in the region. They were driven by the same catastrophic climate changes happening in their home range. These Neolithic newcomers became Europe's first farmers and herders. They arrived from the southeast of Eurasia bringing domesticated plants and animals as well as an entirely new lifestyle to Northern Europe. In studying the mitochondrial DNA of early hunter-gatherer burials and those of early agriculturalists, a team from Mainz University in Germany, together with researchers from University College London and Cambridge, have found that the first farmers in central and Northern Europe were immigrants from the east and that the European gene pool eventually became a mixture of the two groups.[13] The final adoption of farming practices in the outlying bastions of hunting and gathering in Scandinavia and the Baltic was most likely a result of this cultural mixing.[14]

For the ancestors living in a time of such catastrophic climatic shifts followed by the dramatic cultural changes brought by the new immigrants, it would be highly advantageous to carry memories beyond the lifetime of a few generations. Stories of the past and of past events would have been dear treasures that would have helped to provide the people a sense of home and belonging. Stories would have also been used to preserve the memory of traumatic events—such as the loss of ancestral lands—in an effort to predict and so prevent future calamities. I can imagine that in the face of so much change, there would have been an urgent need to tell stories to safeguard the people's sense of identity. Stories would have been told with the purpose of memorizing and so perpetuating the wisdom of the remaining elders.

Information preserved in oral culture and myth can be amazingly long-lived. On the Indonesian island of Flores, the Ngadha and Manggarai tribes tell stories about short, hairy people called the Ebu Gogo. These "mythical" creatures have anatomical features that sound remarkably like those of *Homo floresiensis*. This is the name given to the species whose fossil remains were found on the island. If this myth represents a retained cultural memory, it would be at least 12,000 years old, as that is the time period when *Homo floresiensis* became extinct.[15]

The Aboriginal people of Australia have "songlines" or "dreaming tracks" that have survived for tens of millennia. They are said to

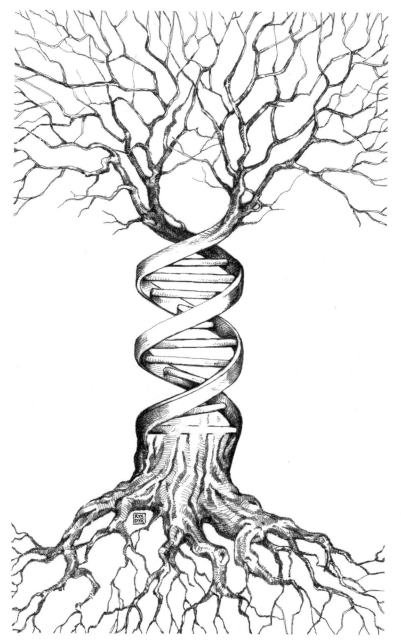

Figure 2.3. DNA is a self-replicating molecule that is the basis of nearly all organisms living on Earth. Thanks to the Human Genome Project, we know that our DNA carries genetic information from all our hominid ancestors. There are also sections of our genetic code that we share with other creatures. For instance, we have a common ancestor with every animal that has a backbone and also with more surprising creatures such as sea urchins and starfish, as we share a common ancestor with them, too!

describe the paths the creator beings of the primordial "Dreamtime" took across the land. These songs have been preserved so accurately that a knowledgeable person is able to navigate across the land by repeating the words of the song. These songlines accurately describe the location of landmarks, water holes, and other natural phenomena across the entire continent. In North America, scholars have debated for over two centuries about the idea that memories of extinct Pleistocene megafauna, such as woolly mammoths, were preserved for thousands of years in the folktales of the Northern Algonquin people and in the legends of the Kaska of central British Columbia.

Along with stories, peoples in oral cultures from the Arctic to the far Pacific have used string figures, which are complex versions of the childhood "cat's cradle" game, as mnemonic devices supporting an accurate linear transmission of mythic narratives. Rather than just relying on mental memory, the string figures make use of muscle memory to assist in preserving an accurate, linear telling of cultural stories. Among the Inuit people, a string figure representing a large creature has been identified as the long-extinct mammoth.[16]

Oral traditions can also reflect shifting social values and other cultural changes. Some aspects of oral narratives conform to current political and social realities of their communities, while others resist revision and remain historically valid, scrupulously preserved features of orally transmitted memory. Together, these elements of oral evidence provide both immutable and historically dynamic cultural memory.[17]

The paradigm-changing events our human ancestors on every continent endured were so extraordinarily momentous that they must have preserved these experiences in their stories for subsequent generations. Is it possible that echoes of Stone Age history could have remained in the myths of the people of the North for thousands of years until the age of the Vikings? I believe it is and that Old Norse mythology preserved threads of our communal ancestors' shamanic spirituality, their ancient anxiety about catastrophic change, and the subsequent generations' responses to immigration and shifting lifestyle patterns.

◈ *Using Fire to Meet a Shamanic Ancestor*

This is an opportunity to journey with your drum or rattle while being with the fire. In this way, you are giving yourself an experience that can help to connect with your shamanic ancestors.

For this exercise, you will need:

- Either a safe outdoor fire ring or indoor fireplace
- Tinder, kindling, and firewood for a sacred fire
- Matches or other ignition source
- Your rattle or drum
- Offering materials
- Some of your favorite food
- Your journal or a notebook and pen
- A safe way to extinguish the fire should an emergency arise

◈ Making the Journey

1. Choose a time when you will be able to spend a few hours with the fire until it goes completely out.
2. Prepare yourself and all the materials as you did in the previous exercise. Once preparations are complete, honor the spirits of all directions and ask them to bless the area where you will be working.
3. Now call your power animal to you. This spirit will protect your body and also accompany you on your journey.
4. Next you will make an offering to the spirits of your ancestors. An offering is one way a shaman creates a more concrete connection with spirits. Shamans feed and care for the spirits as they would a loved one. They understand the importance of developing and maintaining reverent participatory relationships with nature, the spirits, and their ancestors.

    It is best to make your offering outdoors even if your fire is to be made inside. Begin to rattle or drum softly for a few minutes. While you are rattling or drumming, imagine the incredibly long line of shamanic ancestors standing behind you. You may see them by their fire; they may be dancing; they might have drums, rattles, or healing herbs; and they may be singing. Thank them in advance for their assistance in working with the fire by making your offering. Take a small bit of your favorite food and place it on the ground. Eat a small bit of this same food yourself in communion with them.

5. Once you have made your offering to the ancestors, make an offering in the fireplace or on the ground in the fire ring that will receive the fire. Thank the place for holding the fire for you by making an offering.

6. Now set up a small fire, but do not light it yet. Once the kindling and firewood are ready to receive the match, begin rattling softly. Remember the ancestors and begin to hum or tone from your heart.

7. Let the fire know that you are seeking to meet your shamanic ancestors. Then light the fire. As the wood begins to catch, sing more loudly with the intent of honoring the ancestors' spirits with your song. To show gratitude to the fire spirit for working with you, toss a small bit of offering material into the flames to feed it.

8. When the fire is full, sit as close to it as you can safely, rattle or drum softly, and gaze deeply into the fire. Allow the fire spirit to introduce you to your ancestors. You may see images in the flames, you may hear their voices whispering to you or you may feel their presence. The ancestors will communicate with your heart in their own way. As the fire dies to coals, it will continue to provide information and connection, so it is important to stay with the fire until it completely goes out. As the embers cool, begin to record your impressions of the experience in your journal.

9. When through, make another offering to the ancestors and the fire for their loving assistance.

On the next morning when you are sure the last of the coals are completely cold, save a bit of the ashes in a special place. You may place the ashes on your altar, put a pinch in your medicine bag, or place a small bowl of these ashes in a favorite place in your home. This is a way to honor the moment you were able to connect with your shamanic ancestor. As you did in the previous exercise, take a bit more ash and mix it with cornmeal or flour to sprinkle on the earth. Again thank the ancestors, the fire, the air, the wood, and the earth for their gifts.

You may have a very clear idea of what you learned or may have to sit with the experience for a while to understand what you were given. Allow your heart to receive the gifts.

◈ **Other Journey Explorations**

- ◆ Journey to a teacher or power animal to ask them to take you to your shamanic ancestor. Once you meet them, thank them for making you possible! Introduce yourself and ask the ancestor, "What is your name?" Once you know his name, ask him, "How can we begin to work together?" This spirit can become a powerful teacher for you. Record the content of your journey and your perceptions about what you received.

- ◆ Journey to a teacher or power animal to ask, "What is the most important thing I gained from being with my shamanic ancestor?" Record the content of your journey and your perceptions about what you received

- ◆ Journey to your shamanic ancestor: "How did you use fire to perceive the spirit realms?"

- ◆ Journey to your shamanic ancestor: "How did you understand the spirit world?"

After each journey, thank your power animal, your teacher, and your ancestor. Then make an offering to the spirits.

◈ **Process Questions**

- ◆ Write down in your journal what it was like to be with the fire.

- ◆ What was it like to meet your shamanic ancestor? Write down all that you felt.

- ◆ How does it feel to have begun a relationship with your ancestors? Record your impressions.

◎ ◎ ◎

It is important to nurture an ongoing relationship with this ancestor. She is a vital link to your personal shamanic past. Continue making journeys to this ancestor to ask how you can learn more about her understanding of the world, how she understood her relationships with the spirits, and most importantly how you may continue to honor her for her teachings.

3

Power in the Female Body

In her book *The Woman in the Shaman's Body*, Barbara Tedlock argues that the prehistoric foundations of our species' shamanic activity is filled with evidence that women have been important and active participants in those practices. She highlights convincing pieces of evidence that reveal prehistoric women shamans. One of these is the skeleton that was unearthed in Dolni Věstonice.[1]

Dolni Věstonice is an Upper Paleolithic archaeological site in the Czech Republic about 100 miles north of Vienna, Austria. First discovered in the early twentieth century, the site was radiocarbon dated to approximately 28,000 years ago. While this place is now arguably near the geographic center of Europe, during the Upper Paleolithic period the area was on the edge of the glacial ice. A skeleton unearthed there was of a woman in her forties—old enough to have been a grandparent. As an elder, she would have been important to her people. Rachel Caspari argues that elderly people were highly influential in prehistoric society.[2] Grandparents assisted in childcare, perpetuated cultural transmission through storytelling, and contributed to the increased complexity of stone tools through their practiced experience. In other words, during the Stone Age, elders were a vital repository of all the collected knowledge, history, and wisdom of their people.

Not simply set apart by her advanced years, the skull of the woman of Dolni Věstonice revealed that she also had a marked facial asymmetry. Her high-status burial and facial deformity suggests that she was a shaman. According to Brian Hayden, an archaeologist at Simon Fraser University, people with disabilities were often thought to have unusual or supernatural power.[3] This special woman was buried under two engraved mammoth shoulder blades. She and the contents of her grave had been painted with red ochre after her death. Over her head was a flint spearhead, and in one hand she held the body of a fox.

Twelve thousand years ago in another part of Eurasia, a shaman in what is now northern Israel was afforded similar honors when she was interred.[4] Relatively old for her time, the nearly 5-foot-tall, 45-year-old woman was placed in a mud-plastered and rock-lined pit in a cave and was buried beneath a large stone slab. She was buried with fifty carefully arranged tortoise shells; parts of wild pigs; an eagle wing; a cow tail; a leopard's pelvis; two marten skulls; the forearm of a wild boar, which was laid in alignment with her upper left arm; and other artifacts, including a human foot.*

Approximately 9,000 years ago, a younger female shaman was interred in a foot-thick layer of red ochre in what is now Bad Dürrenberg, Germany. Like her predecessors, she was interred with many extraordinary grave goods, including crane, beaver, and deer bones, as well as antlers and shells. She was also accompanied by a year-old child. Entering the spirit realms for the final time, she wore her shamanic costume (see figure 3.2, page 42). A spray of feathers was attached to her right shoulder. Over her leather dress, she wore a deerskin cape with the face of the deer drawn up over her head as a hood. Antlers were affixed to the top. A breastplate of leather and split boar tusks hung on her chest, and the area above her eyes and around her face was lavishly decorated with suspended slices of boar tusks and other animal bones and teeth. Along her brow, a fringe mask or "eye curtain" of beads and ruminant incisors dangled in front of her eyes.[5] This toothy mask was very similar to the bead and leather fringe

---

*This last inclusion is especially interesting, as the woman would have limped and dragged one of her own feet as she walked because of a spinal deformity.

Figure 3.1. This thumb-sized mammoth tusk carving of the Dolni Věstonice shaman is the oldest representation of an individual person found to date.

masks that are still worn by the shamans of Siberia and Central Asia.

Throughout northern Eurasian cultures, shamans were frequently women.[6] The shaman's grave of Dolni Věstonice has many similarities to others found across the region that range in dates from the Upper Paleolithic to a much more recent past. In the far-eastern Russian Arctic, a grave from only 2,000 years ago and dating from the Old Bering Sea culture held the skeleton of an elderly woman with a wooden mask at her knees. Her grave had been constructed so that she appeared to have been

Figure 3.2. The shaman of Bad Dürrenburg was buried in her shamanic regalia. (Pen and ink ©2016 Evelyn C. Rysdyk after a reconstruction by Karol Schauer for LDA Sachsen-Anhalt.)

Figure 3.3. This Evenk shaman's cap is designed in the
same style as a woman's traveling cap. Siberian shaman
costumes also feature forms that include aprons and long dresses
that are similar to the tribal groups' traditional female clothing.

laid to rest in the body of a whale. Many of the artifacts found in this
grave are objects that would have been used in women's activities; however,
her grave also held objects related to healing, rituals, and dance, indicating
that this woman was most probably a shaman. From the wide varieties of
burial offerings in her grave, it was also clear that her people revered her.

During the early twentieth century prior to the Soviet Revolution,
the cultural anthropologist M. A. Czaplicka gathered together much
of the remaining shamanic knowledge of Siberian tribes. In her 1914
book *Aboriginal Siberia: A Study in Social Anthropology,* she quotes a

Chukchee proverb, "Woman is by nature a shaman." Indeed, hunter-gatherer tribes across the Arctic, Siberia, and Central and Eastern Asia preserved the tradition that the prototypical First Shaman was female. It is for that reason that both male and female shamans' ceremonial costumes reflect traditional women's garments, such as aprons, skirts, and caps. Czaplicka said it this way, "Taking into account the present prominent position of female shamans among many Siberian tribes and their place in traditions, together with certain feminine attributes of the male shaman (such as dress, habits, privileges) and certain linguistic similarities between the names for male and female shamans . . . in former days, only female shamans existed, and . . . the male shaman is a later development."[7]

This information is not meant to suggest in any way that men cannot be shamans or that male shamans didn't exist in prehistory! Rather it is to suggest that a primeval female archetype is central to the deepest roots of the tradition. In venerating the feminine as a source of power, perhaps the people of prehistory were acknowledging that we have all come into this world from a womb and that our species—indeed all species—were born from the body of Mother Earth. Her elements make our physical life possible, and a deep connection with the natural world—with Mother Nature in all her magnificence and abundance—is at the heart of shamanic spirituality.

Within the Earth's sacred embrace, masculine and feminine energies dance together for the continuance of life. New generations of human beings and other creatures are born from this dance. Each new being is then nurtured by the Earth's air, her water, her plants, and her animals. When our physical lives are over, we return again to her body. She is pivotal to the sacred circle of existence.

AN ASSURANCE OF ABUNDANCE

Evidence suggests that the Upper Paleolithic shaman from Dolni Věstonice was also a potter. This shaman was fashioning and firing

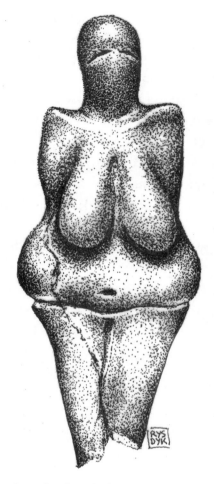

Figure 3.4. This female figure found during the
Dolni Věstonice excavation is the oldest known ceramic
object in the world, predating the advent of pottery vessels
by thousands of years.

clay thousands of years before any other pottery vessels were made. She created many ceramic* figurines of animals and one particular figure that resembled other so-called Venus statues of the time period. These prehistoric statuettes of women portrayed with similar robust physical

---

*The fired-clay figures at this site predate any other ceramic technology by more than 14,000 years.[8]

attributes have been found in Europe and as far east as Irkutsk Oblast, Siberia, near Lake Baikal. The earliest figure found in Hohle Fels near Schelklingen, Germany, was dated to approximately 40,000 years ago. These figures continued to be made all across Eurasia.

More recent finds in northern France and Romania* (6,000 years old), a sandstone figure† discovered near Kakinada in the East-Central region of India (5,000 years old), and another from the Old Bering Sea culture (2,000 years old) reveal that our ancestors continued creating these mother/grandmother images in bone, ivory, stone, and clay for over 38,000 years. That equates to at least 1,900 generations! For any cultural idea to be transmitted so consistently from one generation to the next for so many thousands of years, it had to have been considered vitally essential to the culture.

A recent study published in the *Journal of Anthropology* suggests that the figures constitute evidence that a shared cultural tradition existed across northern Eurasia from the time period of the Upper Paleolithic cave painters and persisted into the period when the first megalithic structures were being constructed in the region.[9] Given that most of the figures were created during the extremely challenging climatic conditions that prevailed at this time, it seems likely that only a very few women survived to become elders and fewer still to be as corpulent as is depicted by many of the figurines. Therefore, these portable images of very well-nourished, multiparous‡ mature females may have been talismans for success in the very difficult struggle to survive and reproduce.[10] In this way, the figures can be seen as related to shamanic doll-like effigies used by Siberian tribes until the twentieth century that

---

*The artifact was from the *Cucuteni-Trypillian* culture, also known as *Cucuteni* culture (from Romanian), *Trypillian* culture (from Ukrainian), or *Tripolye* culture (from Russian), which is a Neolithic/Copper Age archaeological culture that existed from approximately 4800 to 3000 BCE, from the Carpathian Mountains to what is now modern-day Romania, Moldova, and Ukraine.

†The Mother Goddess was found by archaeologists outside of the Sri Chalukya Kumara Bheemeswara Swamy temple at Samarlakota near Kakinada in East Godavari district of Andhra Pradesh.

‡Meaning a woman that would have borne more than one child.

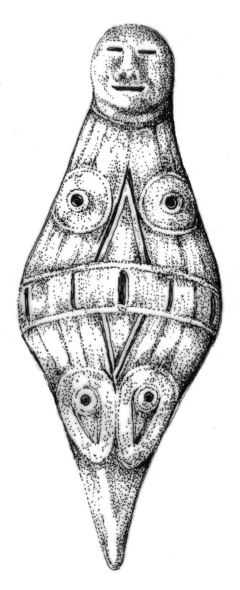

Figure 3.5. This walrus ivory ceremonial ladle handle featuring a "Venus" from the Old Bering Sea culture was excavated in Ekven, an archaeological site in the Russian Chukotka Autonomous Okrug.

were used to protect the people from calamities such as disease, famine, or injury. Like those effigies, these female figures may have functioned as spiritual containers that held the essence or spirit of the symbolic mother/grandmother—a symbol of bounty, fertility, protection, and wisdom. In other words, these figures may well have been talismans to ensure survival, longevity, and tribal continuance.

The spiritual image of elder females lasted for nearly four hundred centuries. Shaman graves tell us that particularly gifted women were also honored. Since these ideas persisted for so long, one can imagine that even after a few generations, they would have formed part of the culture's primordial past. In other words, a female holy image and the female shaman would have been concepts that had "always been so."

◈ *Journeying to Meet the First Shaman*

This is an opportunity to meet the mother of all shamans. The journey will be with your power animal to your shamanic ancestor. Ask that ancestor to take you to the first person to intentionally work with the spirits on behalf of her people.

As you did before, you may use the fire to connect with your ancestral shaman. If that isn't possible, by all means feel empowered to journey with a drum, a rattle, or a shamanic drumming recording that includes a callback signal.

For this exercise, you will need:

- Either a safe outdoor fire ring or indoor fireplace
- Tinder, kindling, and firewood for a sacred fire
- Matches or other ignition source
- Your rattle or drum
- Offering materials
- Some of your favorite food
- Your journal or a notebook and pen
- A safe way to extinguish the fire in an emergency

◈ Making the Journey

1. Choose a time when you will be able to spend a few hours with the fire until it goes completely out. If you are not planning to use the fire to journey, then make sure you have a quiet place to have a long, uninterrupted time with the spirits.

2. Prepare yourself and all the materials as you did in the previous exercise. (If you do plan to use a fire, follow the directions for honoring it that you did when you met your shamanic ancestor.) Once preparations are complete, honor the spirits of all directions, and ask them to bless the area where you will be working.

3. Now call your power animal to you. This spirit will protect your body and also accompany you on your journey.

4. Next you will make an offering to the spirits of your ancestors. An offering is one way a shaman creates a more concrete connection with spirits. Shamans feed and care for the spirits as they would a loved one. They understand the importance of developing and maintaining reverent participatory relationships with nature, the spirits, and their ancestors.

   As you did before, make your offering outdoors even if you are going to be journeying inside. Begin to rattle or drum softly for a few minutes. While you are rattling or drumming, imagine the incredibly long line of shamanic ancestors standing behind you. You may see them by their fire; they may be dancing; they might have drums, rattles, or healing herbs; and they may be singing. Thank them in advance for their assistance in working with the fire by making your offering. Take a small bit of your favorite food and place it on the ground. Eat a small bit of this same food yourself in communion with them.

5. Once you have made your offering to the ancestors, take time to connect with your rattle or drum. Thank the place in which you plan to journey for holding you. Use whatever materials you normally use for making an offering.

6. Now begin rattling softly. Remember the ancestors, and begin to hum or tone from your heart.

7. Hold a strong intention to again meet with your shamanic ancestor. Keeping this intention, sing more loudly with the intent of honoring the ancestors' spirits with your song.

8. When you meet your shamanic ancestor, greet him and ask him to take you to the very first shaman—the Mother Shaman of us all.

9. When you meet the First Shaman, introduce yourself and ask how she prefers to be addressed. Tell her about who you are and most importantly what is in your heart. Honor that being for beginning the path that you chose to follow.

10. When you feel complete, be sure to thank him, your shamanic ancestor, and your power animal. If you worked with fire, make sure to thank the fire spirit, too. Return fully to ordinary consciousness. Once you feel fully back from your journey, make another offering to the ancestors and shamanic helpers for their loving assistance.

You may have a very clear idea of what you learned or you may have to sit with the experience for a while to understand what you were given. Allow your heart to receive the gifts.

◈ Other Journey Explorations

- Visit the First Shaman again in a journey with your shamanic ancestor and your power animal. Once you meet her, ask how you may begin learning from her.
- Journey to a teacher or power animal to ask, "What is the most important thing I gained from being with the First Shaman?" Record the content of your journey and your perceptions about what you received
- Journey to your shamanic ancestor: "How did you honor the First Shaman?"
- Journey to your shamanic ancestor: "What stories did you learn about the beginnings of shamanism?"
- Journey to your shamanic ancestor: "Please take me to meet more of my shamanic ancestors."

After each journey, thank your power animal, your teacher, your shamanic ancestor, and the First Shaman. Then make an offering to the spirits.

◈ **Process Questions**

- ◆ Write down in your journal what it was like to be with the very first shaman. Write down all that you felt.
- ◆ How has the relationship with your shamanic ancestor begun to shift your perceptions?
- ◆ How does it feel to be developing a shamanic lineage? Record your impressions.

4

Worlds of the Shaman

Around the globe, shamans describe the spiritual realms as places. It is a way to translate the numinous world of the spirit into something within which we can travel by shifting our awareness. In essence, these realms are both actual places and metaphoric representations of states of being that are not physical but rather outside of both time and space. Since our minds have no easy way to relate to what is beyond the three-dimensional world, the journey experience provides us with a kind of bridge between our ordinary reality and that timeless and formless reality. While shamanic journeys may be thought of as metaphoric experiences, they also produce actual and concretely useful information.

Shamans all around the world also seem to travel to similar places on their journeys. It is as though there is a kind of consensual shamanic reality that gives human consciousness the ability to accept and process the material that is received in the journey state. This consensual shamanic reality and its imagery provide a kind of translation service from the intangible, nonlocal plane that exists beyond time and space constraints and our ordinary way of perceiving.

Typically, this consensual shamanic reality or spirit world is divided into levels. These are generally seen as the Upper World, Middle World, and Lower World, (see fig. 1.2 on page 17), although each of these worlds can have many dimensions or levels within them. All of the realms are linked by an axis mundi or great tree. This central column provides a way for the shaman to travel from one realm to the next and provides a unifying field that holds all realities together.

While the spirits who inhabit each of these realms and the types of content available to the individual shaman in each of them will differ from one culture to the next, there are still some similarities.

Middle World is the spiritual aspect of the world in which we live. It holds the spirits of nature, including animals, trees, birds, plants, and insects, as well as the elements of earth, air, fire, and water. This realm is also where one can interact with the spirits of landscape features such as waterfalls, rocks, rivers, and mountains and the spirits of weather such as the rain, winds, lightning, and storms. Transcendent, human-form spiritual teachers may also reside there. It is the fruitful realm of all living beings—the place of tangible form where the nonlocal world of vibration can manifest into the physicality of our sensory experience. This sensory world can be so persuasive that it becomes difficult for some humans to leave it when they die. For this reason the spirits of wandering dead who haven't completed their departure from us also inhabit the Middle World.

Traveling down below the Middle World accesses Lower Worlds. Many shamans describe these as places of primordial vitality where the ancestral spirits of all life on Earth reside. Many shamans suggest that it is where the original spiritual template of each species resides. While we have the spirits of many black bears in the Middle World, the black bear spirit in the Lower Worlds may be perceived as the first one that nurtures and begets all the rest. In keeping with these ancestral themes, for some shamanic cultures the Lower Worlds include the realm of deceased human ancestors. Unlike the dead in the Middle World, these ancestors in the Lower Worlds may be contacted to provide guidance and support to the living.

While the sky is believed to be infinite in depth, shamans nevertheless believe that there are realms beyond the heavens. Going upward and passing through the ordinary sky reaches the shamanic Upper Worlds. They are realms held in the branches of the World Tree and are typically described as being more ethereal in nature. For some cultures, the

Upper Worlds are home for transcendent, human-form spiritual teachers. For the Mongols, the sky world is a brilliant place devoid of inhabitants. An Upper World is where Ulchi shamans keep safe the souls of their patients, and an Upper World is also where shamans in some Siberian cultures believe that a sky deity resides.

The ancient Norse World Tree, Yggdrasil, embraces nine realms, which have parallels to the usual three.* In the tree's uppermost branches was Æsgard, the home of the sky deities. This would be akin to the shamanic Upper World. Five realms are connected around the trunk of Yggdrasil and constitute the Norse Middle World. Close to the center is the human realm, Midgard. Just beyond the human realm are four other realms in the cardinal directions. In the North is Niflheim, the primordial realm of ice and cold. In the South is Muspellheim, the realm of primordial heat and fire. The East is the home of the *jötunn,* the gigantic predecessors of the gods. Their realm is Jötunnheim. In the West lies Vanaheim, the goddess Freyja's center of influence and the home of the nature deities of the earth, waters, and sea.

Just above and below these realms lie "between places" that are more closely aligned with the Middle World. Ljossalheim lies just above but still below Æsgard. It is the realm of the light elves and spirits of the air. Just below lies Svartalfheim, the realm of the black elves or dwarves and the stone spirits.

The Lower World is the realm of Hel, the goddess of the dead. Her home is called Helheim and also referred to as Hel. This place is also the home of deceased ancestors. Because the nature of the soul[†] is tripartite in Norse cosmology, one part of the soul retains the personality

---

*Nine is a sacred number for many tribes in Siberia. There are nine notches in the birch tree or larch tree that is climbed by shamanic initiates all across the Siberian taiga. Similar trees are climbed as one would a ladder to access the spiritual realms.

†Soul plurality is a common belief across the north. Similar ideas about the human soul having three aspects are observed across Siberia and Central Asia. The Evenks, Nenets, Enets, Nganasans, Selkups, Mongolians, Buryats, Khakas, and Finnic cultures all share the belief of a tripartite soul. The Inupiaq, Yup'ik, and Aleut of North America believe in two souls, with a third soul that manifests once a person is named.

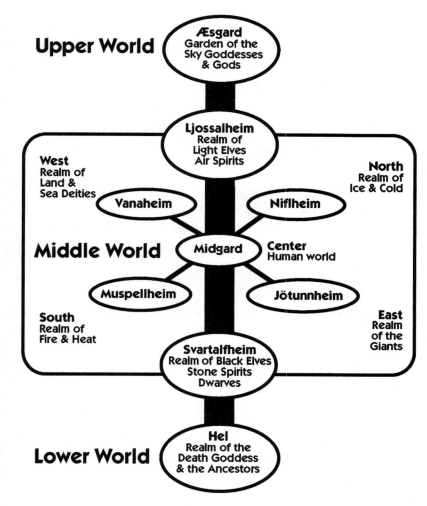

Figure 4.1. This diagram of Yggdrasil shows how the nine spirit worlds of the Old Norse relate to the usual three worlds of shamanism.

and resides in this realm. These ancestral spirits are consulted in shamanic ritual to offer guidance and wisdom.

Of course, spiritual experiences are nonlinear and nonlocal in nature. Compartmentalized delineations of the spiritual landscape assist us in the sensory, three-dimensional world to more easily receive wisdom from the asomatous plane of the spirits. The spirits themselves travel freely through these realms.

To better understand the Norse cosmological landscape it is best to have your own experiences of the nine realms. In having your own experience, you will gain a visceral understanding of the relationship between the realms and the World Tree that connects them.

◈ *Journeying to Explore the Nine Realms of Spirit*

This is an opportunity to have personal experiences of the realms. It is recommended that you do separate journeys for each of the nine realms. Have your power animal guide you and either your shamanic ancestor or the First Shaman travel with you on each of the journeys. As you did before, you may use the fire to connect with your ancestral shaman. If that isn't possible, by all means feel empowered to journey with a drum, a rattle, or a shamanic drumming recording that includes a callback signal.

For this exercise, you will need:

- Either a safe outdoor fire ring or indoor fireplace
- Tinder, kindling, and firewood for a sacred fire
- Matches or other ignition source
- Your rattle or drum
- Offering materials
- Some of your favorite food
- Your journal or a notebook and pen
- A safe way to extinguish the fire in an emergency

◈ Making the Journey

1. Choose a time when you will be able to spend a few hours with the fire until it goes completely out. If you are not planning to use the fire to journey, then make sure you have a quiet place to have a long, uninterrupted time with the spirits.

2. Prepare yourself and all the materials as you did in the previous exercise. (If you do plan to use a fire, follow the directions for honoring it that

you did when you met your shamanic ancestor.) Once preparations are complete, honor the spirits of all directions, and ask them to bless the area where you will be working.

3. Now call your power animal to you. This spirit will protect your body and also accompany you on your journey.

4. Next you will make an offering to the spirits of your ancestors. An offering is one way a shaman creates a more concrete connection with spirits. Shamans feed and care for the spirits as they would a loved one. They understand the importance of developing and maintaining reverent participatory relationships with nature, the spirits, and their ancestors.

   As you did before, make your offering outdoors even if you are going to be journeying inside. Begin to rattle or drum softly for a few minutes. While you are rattling or drumming, imagine the incredibly long line of shamanic ancestors standing behind you. You may see them by their fire; they may be dancing; they might have drums, rattles, or healing herbs; and they may be singing. Thank them in advance for their assistance in working with the fire by making your offering. Take a small bit of your favorite food and place it on the ground. Eat a small bit of this same food yourself in communion with them.

5. Once you have made your offering to the ancestors, take time to connect with your rattle or drum. Thank the place in which you plan to journey for holding you. Use whatever materials you normally use for making an offering.

6. Now begin rattling or drumming softly. Remember the ancestors, and begin to hum or tone from your heart.

7. Invite your shamanic ancestor or the First Shaman to accompany you into the realm you wish to explore.

8. Enter the World Tree, and travel to your intended destination.

9. Have your power animal and accompanying spirit support you to have a personal experience of the realm.

10. When you feel complete, be sure to thank the spirits you interacted with. If you worked with fire, make sure to thank the fire spirit, too.

Return fully to ordinary consciousness. Once you feel fully back from your journey, make another offering to the ancestors and shamanic helpers for their loving assistance.

You may have a very clear idea of what you learned or you may have to sit with the experience for a while to understand what you were given. Allow your heart to receive the gifts by giving yourself ample time to reflect on your journey.

◈ Other Journey Explorations

- Journey to each realm to meet a "spokesperson" from that world to help you understand the nature of the spirits in that place.
- Journey to a teacher or power animal to ask, "What do I need to understand about the nine realms?" Record the content of your journey and your perceptions about what you received.
- Journey to your shamanic ancestor: "What is the relationship between Muspellheim and Niflheim?"
- Journey to your shamanic ancestor: "How are Ljossalheim and Svartalfheim connected to Middle World?"

After each journey, thank your power animal, your teacher, your shamanic ancestor, and the First Shaman. Then make an offering to the spirits.

◈ Process Questions

- Write down in your journal what it was like to be in each of the realms. Write down all that you felt.
- How have the experiences in your journeys begun to shift your perceptions about the nine realms? Record your impressions.

5

The First Shaman
Becomes a Goddess

As I shared earlier, Venus artifacts representing a matricentric sense of the divine were made by our ancestors for over 38,000 years. The practice of creating these mother figures continued in northwestern Eurasia until 6,000 years ago and 2,000 years ago in the far eastern regions. This time period coincides with the ending of the Neolithic Age in Northern Europe.

As time passed from the Neolithic into the Chalcolithic or Copper Age, rudimentary farming practices began to spread northwest in Europe. Proto-Indo-European tribes from Anatolia (a region that is now Turkey) began spreading early farming practices into the region approximately 8,000 to 9,500 years ago. This roughly coincides with the period when Doggerland was lost under the ocean. The people affected by the loss of their lands must have begun shifting their seasonal hunting and gathering routes in response to the changes in animal migrations due to the dramatic climate changes during this period. These calamitous transformations of the landscape would have also impacted the peoples across the length and breadth of Eurasia. It may have been the reason that the farming peoples and later pastoralists from the eastern steppes began to move north and westward. From archaeological and linguistic evidence, it is clear that people living a hunting and gathering lifestyle would have begun meeting farmers and herders in what is now central Europe.

The Proto-Indo-Europeans entering into the area from the east practiced pantheism. They had a large retinue of gods and goddesses who were thought to administer or control aspects of daily life and nature. This echoes the cultural framework of farmers who oversee and shape one piece of land for their food and also the cultural patterns of pastoralists whose lifestyle demands protecting, breeding, and controlling the movements of livestock. This is very different from the lifestyle of hunters and gatherers whose survival depends upon moving in harmony with the seasonal migrations of animals, birds, and fish.

From the remnants preserved in myths from the far north of Europe, it is clear to me that this intersection of cultures must have been tremendously difficult. For instance, in the Old Norse pantheon there are two distinct families of divinities. The Æsir are led by the chief sky god Óðinn. They live in their home Æsgard at the top of the central pillar or World Tree that unites all the realms of existence. In shamanic terms, we could think of these deities residing in Upper World.

The other family of gods and goddesses reside in what a shaman would refer to as Middle World. The Vanir are deities associated with untamed nature, fertility, animals, wisdom, the cycle of life/death/rebirth, and the ability to see into the unseen realms. The Vanir are consistently referred to as wise throughout the Icelandic Edda texts and are also referred to as "The Giving Ones." Their home, Vanaheim, was believed to be to the west of Midgard, the realm of human life.

The chief Vanir deity is named Njörðr who is the god of sea, winds, and prosperity. When the Æsir god Óðinn asks the giant Vafþrúðnir about the origins of Njörðr, the giant reveals that he was created in Vanaheim by "wise powers." It is important to note here that jötunn, or giants, predate both the Vanir and Æsir deities. These primordial beings were formed from the elemental chaos that existed before the creation of other matter. The story of a primordial giant is common to the Norse, Greek, and Hindu cosmologies and so most likely has its origins in Proto-Indo-European mythology. Many of these myths suggest that the earth and sky were formed from the body of a slain giant.* Since giants predate the Æsir or Vanir deities and even the world itself, the jötunn carry more ancient wisdom and more primeval powers than the gods or goddesses who are said to have created human beings. This explains why many stories in Norse mythology reveal that the gods and goddesses are fearful of the giants. In spite of their awesome power, most of these beings also live in an aspect of Middle World known as Jötunnheim.

Njörðr is the father of two children. Njörðr was said to have brought these children forth with an unnamed sister. At other places in the myths, he is married to a giant. This suggests that his children are born from the wisdom and chthonic feminine energy in the western land of Vanaheim.

One of Njörðr's children is Freyr, who was associated with sacred rule, virility, sunshine, and fair weather. He lives in and oversees Ljossalheim, a betwixt realm that lies between the high Æsgard and Midgard that is the home of the light elves. These beings may be thought of as having similarities to transcendent Middle World nature spirits like faeries who participate in the vitality of nature. Freyr is typically pictured as a phallic fertility god who eventually woos and marries an incredibly beautiful jötunn goddess named Gerðr. Gerðr's name has been etymologically associated with the earth and so the wedding of her and Freyr is commonly seen as a coupling of fertility and the earth or soil.† Following this logic, the Earth's fertility may be seen as a product of the western lands, as well.

The Vanir deities' mysteriously primordial origins, their identifications with natural phenomena or forces, and the location of their

---

*For the Norse, that first being is a giant named Ymir. In the Rigveda of Hinduism, Purusha is described as a primeval giant that is sacrificed by the gods and from whose body the world is built. The primordial giant Ouranos of Greek mythology presents a similar archetype.

†Good basic information on all of the Norse deities may be found in John Lindow's book, *Norse Mythology: A Guide to the Gods, Heroes, Rituals, and Beliefs.*

homeland suggest that this clan of goddesses and gods may reflect a memory of the nature-centered spirituality practiced in Europe before the arrival of the Proto-Indo-European people. In my opinion, the goddess Freyja provides reinforcement to this idea.

The goddess Freyja is also a child of Njörðr. She is the goddess of love, beauty, sexuality, war, death, healing, magic, and prophesy. Associated with cats, a boar, and falcons, she is a mistress of the animals. In her role as a goddess of sex, love, and battle, she is the life giver and death dealer. As the goddess of magic and prophesy, she is the one who can see what others cannot. Since in Indo-European traditions, the gods and goddesses are thought to be the progenitors of human beings, Freyja's roles seem to position her as a descendant of the primeval divine female or goddess.* At the same time, her knowledge of healing and ability to divine mystic knowledge also suggest that she exists as the remembered archetype of the First Shaman. Snorri[†] wrote, in his Icelandic *Ynglingasaga,* that the daughter of Njörðr was Freyja and that she was a *gyðja* (priestess) of sacrifices.[1] She was the first to teach *seiðr* (a shamanic, oracular tradition discussed in a later chapter) to the Æsir, such as was custom among the Vanir. We can see her as the first to whom all human Norse shamans also owed their skills.

Freyja does exhibit attributes and actions that can be interpreted as shamanic. First, she operates outside the accepted parameters of other deities. In spite of the myths being written down during the early Christian era in Iceland, Freyja is depicted as expressing her sexuality without regard to the typical social conventions of Viking times. This

---

*There are also parallels with the Proto-Indo-European goddess Plthivi Mh-ter, or "Mother Earth." This goddess is remembered in the Sanskrit language as Prithvi Mata—She who holds everything—that is, all of Life. Mantras are chanted to her to seek her blessings for health, wealth, and nourishment for the self and family, for harmony, for patience, and also for cooperation. Having a thousand aspects, she is also honored so that the worshiper can gain inspiration and develop greater understanding—in other words, see the big picture of a particular circumstance.

†Snorri Sturluson was an Icelandic historian, poet, and politician during the late twelfth and early thirteenth centuries who wrote down the many stories we now refer to as the Icelandic sagas.

Figure 5.1. This silver pendant of the goddess Freyja was found in Tissø, Denmark. In this depiction, she is represented in the act of twisting or pulling her two hair braids. This fierce presentation of the goddess may be to display her in a battle rage or exhorting warriors into battle. Collection of the National Museum of Denmark.

has parallels with shamans often living at the fringes of a community or exhibiting behaviors that set them apart from other people. Their unconventional attitudes are tolerated because of the value shamans provide to the larger society.

One such story of the goddess tells of her dalliance with the dark elves (dwarves), Austri (east), Sudri (south), Vestri (west) and Nordi (north), who hold up the corners of sky formed from the giant Ymir's dismembered skull. Freyja consorts with each of these representatives of the cardinal directions so that she can possess the magical necklace Brisingamen, which glitters like the stars and sun. Union with other-worldly beings is an aspect of how shamans attain power to accomplish their duties. In this case, Freyja merges with the spirits of the four corners of the Earth. Her goal is said to be a physical object, but perhaps since the Old Norse root *brísingr* refers to both "fire" and "amber," it may be that her task was to gather and return streaming sunlight to the world at the end of a dark, northern winter. In essence, she encircles the Earth to bring back the circle of the Sun, represented by the circle of her necklace.

Freyja also performs the art of *hamskipti,* or shape-shifting. She has a cloak of falcon feathers that allows her to fly through the nine realms of the Norse spirit world. In her cloak, she becomes her falcon *fylgja,* or animal ally and spirit helper.* This has parallels to the ways many shamans work. Among the tribes in Siberia, shamans' coats are covered in streamers representing feathers that allow them to "fly" through the spirit worlds. This also represents the shaman's ability to shape-shift into a bird. In addition, she moves between the realms of Midgard, Vanaheim, Svartalfheim, and the sky realm of Æsgard with ease, as a shaman "traveling between the worlds."

The goddess Freyja's close associations with other animals such as the boar and with cats have echoes in the shaman's retinue of animal companions and power animals. Mythology suggests that cats pull her chariot across the sky. Viking cats were not your standard domesticated lap cats but rather a wild breed native to the north. In Danish these cats are called *huldrekat.* Their name refers to the female forest spirits or *huldre/huldra.* These are the "hidden folk" who, like the transcendent Middle World spirits of other cultures, exhibit an appearance that is a blend of human and animal traits. Norse stories describe the huldre having animal tails and backs that are either hollow or covered in bark. As *skogsrå* (female forest keeper) these beings are considered protectors of the woodlands in the same way their sister beings, the *sjörå,* protect lakes and other freshwater, the *havsrå* protect the seas and bays, and the *bergsrå* guard the mountains.

---

*The act of riding a spirit animal or through the use of magical means is called *gandreið* in Old Norse, a word that means "to witch ride" or "riding a chant, incantation, or enchantment."

Perhaps Freyja is actually not transported by cats but accompanied by a retinue of Middle World nature spirits with a blended or shape-shifted appearance. Having such accompaniment would certainly befit her high status and be coherent with her role as Nature/Earth Goddess.

When flying into fray as battle goddess, Freyja sits astride the boar, Hildisvíni. Magical transport is often a role for the shaman's power animal. That her ride is a boar has further significance as according to the Lithuanian-American archaeologist, Marija Gimbutas, the boar and bear retained magical status into the Neolithic period through their associations with the primordial Mother Goddess.

The *Ynglingasaga,* of the Icelandic sagas written down by Snorri Sturluson, suggests that the shamanic visionary ritual of seiðr,* which was originally practiced largely by women, had its origins among the Vanir and specifically with the goddess Freyja. It is she and she alone who can glimpse the patterns of cosmic space, time, and fate.

The Icelandic sagas also reported that Freyja was the only deity to survive the end of the world, and it was said that she held to the practice of making sacrifices; these may have been causally related. In shamanic cultures, rituals of sacrifice and gratitude or feeding the spirits are a primary way of attending to harmony and promoting continued good fortune. In this way, we can see Freyja acting in her role as the shaman by attending to the continuance of Life through ceremonial action.

In her role as Mother Goddess and First Shaman, Freyja would have been primarily responsible for the cycles of the seasons, the rhythms of birth, life, death, and rebirth, as well as the harmonious interplay of nature and the elements. In this way, she has parallels to other earth goddesses found in cultures around the world and throughout time. Freyja is sister to the Hindu goddess Durga, who, in her many aspects, is the goddess of creation, preservation, and annihilation. She has parallels to the ancient Egyptian goddess Isis, who was revered as the patroness

---

*This shamanic practice is discussed at length in later chapters.

of nature and magic, the protector of the dead, and the goddess of children. The Incan goddess Pachamama, the goddess of earth, nature, and time, is also Freyja's sister, as is the Lakota Sioux Unci Maka, or "Grandmother Earth."

As Gimbutas stressed repeatedly in her work, by understanding what the goddess represents, we can better understand nature—as the goddess is the personification of Nature itself. The goddess Freyja was the deity the Old Norse entreated for help with issues of childbirth, fertility of fields, forest, livestock, and human beings, of foresight and prophecy, as well as matters of luck in both love and battle. In other words, Freyja's purview includes the cycles of earthly life as experienced in human time.

Her larger role was as one who keeps harmony, ensuring that the summer will follow spring, dawn will always follow the night, and nature will remain bountiful. She is remembered as the approachable of the deities—one who could be always be called upon for assistance as the Nature Goddess and First Shaman.

◈ Journeying to Meet the Nature Goddess/First Shaman

This is an opportunity to meet the goddess in her form as archetype for all shamans. The journey will be with your power animal to your shamanic ancestor. Ask that ancestor to take you to meet Freyja, or the Nature Goddess/First Shaman in one of her other forms.

As you did before, you may use the fire to connect with your ancestral shaman. If that isn't possible, by all means feel empowered to journey with a drum or rattle or with a shamanic drumming recording that includes a callback signal.

For this exercise, you will need:

- ◆ Your rattle or drum
- ◆ Offering materials
- ◆ Some of your favorite food

- Your journal or a notebook and pen
- Fire-making supplies if you plan to use the fire to support your journey

◈ Making the Journey

1. Choose a time when you will be able to spend a long, uninterrupted time with the spirits.
2. Prepare yourself and all the materials as you did in the previous exercise. Once preparations are complete, honor the spirits of all directions, and ask them to bless the area where you will be working.
3. Now call your power animal to you. This spirit will protect your body and also accompany you on your journey.
4. Next you will make an offering to the spirits of your ancestors as a part of maintaining reverent participatory relationships with them.

   As you did before, make your offering outdoors even if you are going to be journeying inside. Begin to rattle or drum softly for a few minutes. While you are rattling or drumming, imagine the incredibly long line of shamanic ancestors standing behind you. You may see them by their fire; they may be dancing; they might have drums, rattles, or healing herbs; and they may be singing. Thank them in advance for their assistance in working with the fire by making your offering. Take a small bit of your favorite food and place it on the ground. Eat a small bit of this same food yourself in communion with them.
5. Once you have made your offerings and preparations, begin your journey.
6. Hold a strong intention to again meet with your shamanic ancestor. Keeping this intention, honor the spirits with your song.
7. When you meet your shamanic ancestor, greet her and ask her to take you to meet the Earth Goddess/Shaman.
8. When you meet the Nature Goddess/First Shaman, introduce yourself and ask how she prefers to be addressed. Tell her about who you are and most importantly what is in your heart. Honor her for your life, the bounty of nature, and all the elements that create you.

9. If she allows you to ask her a question, ask her what is most important for you to know right now. Receive her teaching in whatever form she chooses to present her answer.

10. When you feel complete, be sure to thank her, your shamanic ancestor, and your power animal. If you worked with fire, make sure to thank the fire spirit, too. Return fully to ordinary consciousness. Once you feel fully back from your journey, make another offering to the ancestors and shamanic helpers for their loving assistance.

Allow yourself time to assimilate what you have learned. While you may have a very clear idea of what you learned, it is also true that sitting with the experience for a while will help you to understand what you were given more deeply.

◈ Other Journey Explorations

- Make a journey with your shamanic ancestor and your power animal again to the Nature Goddess/First Shaman. Once you meet her, ask how you may begin learning from her.
- Journey to a teacher or power animal to ask, "What is the most important thing I gained from being with the Nature Goddess/ Shaman?" Record the content of your journey and your perceptions about what you received.
- Journey to your shamanic ancestor: "How did you honor the Nature Goddess/First Shaman?"
- Journey to your shamanic ancestor: "What stories did you learn about nature from the Nature Goddess/Shaman?
- Journey to your shamanic ancestor: "Please take me to meet more of my shamanic ancestors."

After each journey, thank your power animal, your teacher, your shamanic ancestor, the First Shaman, and the Nature Goddess/First Shaman. Then make an offering to the spirits.

◈ **Process Questions**

- Write down in your journal what it was like to be with the Nature Goddess/First Shaman. Write down all that you felt.
- What did you learn about the cycles of Life from the Nature Goddess/First Shaman?
- How has the relationship with these spirits begun to shift your perceptions?

6

The Norns

Mistresses of Cosmic Patterns

One of a shaman's roles is to intercede with the spirits. It may be to ask the master spirits of game animals to give some of their children to the hunters, it may be to ask the spirits of the rain to swell the rivers, or it may be to ask the plants to provide medicine to the sick. The shaman works with the spirits of the Earth to make life harmonious not only for the people but to preserve life for all beings. The shaman does this with the understanding that all lives are interwoven.

Mythology and folklore may be seen as a way a culture explains the nature of their cosmos. Several key features of Norse myths seem to preserve remnants of the earlier shamanic culture. First, the cosmological landscape of Norse mythology is multileveled. Second, altering consciousness and undertaking a spiritual journey to seek wisdom are pivotal elements for the role of Viking seers and to their god Óðinn, known as a seeker-god because of his efforts to attain knowledge through transformation. Last, female figures have a particularly primal significance—especially in terms of time, cycles, and prophecy.

In her role as the goddess of prophecy, Freyja visits the Norns to discover the patterns that weave the nature of reality. The Norns are mentioned in medieval Icelandic texts. The following lines are from the collection of Old Norse poems known as the *Poetic Edda*. These poems, which were most likely originally part of an oral tradition, were preserved in a thirteenth-century Icelandic manuscript known as the *Konungsbók* or *Codex Regius*. The section below is verses nineteen and twenty from the *Völuspá*, or *Prophecy of the Seeress*.*

19. Ask veit ek standa,
heitir Yggdrasill,
hár baðmr ausinn
hvítaauri,
þaðan koma döggvar
þærs í dala falla,
stendr æ yfir grænn
Urðarbrunni.

19. An ash I know,
Yggdrasil its name,
With water white is
the great tree watered;
Thence come the dews
that fall in the dales [valleys],
Green does it ever grow
by Urðr's well.

20. Þaðan koma meyjar,
margs vitandi,
þrjár ór þeim sæ
er und þolli stendr.
Urð hétu eina,
aðra Verðandi,
skáru á skíði-
Skuld ina þriðju.
Þær lög lögðu,
þær líf kuru
alda börnum,
ørlög seggja.[1]

20. Thence come the maidens
mighty in wisdom,
Three from the dwelling
down 'neath the tree;
Urðr is one named,
Verthandi the next,
On the wood they scored,
and Skuld the third.
Laws they made there,
and life allotted
To the sons of men,
and told their fates.

The maidens that are referred to in the text are the three Norns. These beings are said to be incredibly wise sisters residing at the base of the Norse World Tree, Yggdrasil. They are so powerful that even the gods fear them. Urðr is the eldest, Verðandi the younger, and Skuld the youngest. They reside near a well, a spring, or a freshwater

---

*The translation here is my own and is based on the work done by Paul C. Bauschatz in his *The Well and the Tree: World and Time in Early Germanic Culture* and on Henry Adams Bellows's 1936 translation of *The Poetic Edda*.

sea named Urðarbrunnr. They are responsible for nurturing the Great
Tree that supports and contains all of the realms of spirit and matter.

Joined in action at the foundation that unites and holds all the
realms of reality, the Norns exist outside the influence of the gods,
as they are jötunn. By describing the Norns as jötunn or giantesses, it
means that they were perceived to be primordial beings who predate
all others and so are more powerful than the gods and goddesses. In
other words, while a deity like Freyja held sway over the sky, landscape,
nature, and world of men as the seasons or cycles of Life, the Norns
were responsible for larger patterns that influenced the lives of the gods.
They perceive the patterns that lie beyond both divine and human
awareness. Their status above gods and humans suggests that those that
created these mythic stories perceived the paramount importance of
cosmic cycles. By that I mean those cycles of events that are beyond the
range of human memory or calculations.

Indeed, most of the changes that we experience as sudden and unex-
pected are not actually anomalous or abnormal. More often than not,
we have the evidence that they are either so unpredictably irregular in
their occurrence or repeated in cycles that are so long they are beyond
the collective memory range of the people who experience them.[2]

Given the scope of the cataclysms that our ancestors experienced,
this makes complete sense. In order to come to terms with such catastrophes, it would have been important to believe that some form of
universal order existed. How else could large-scale and chaos-producing
events like wild swings in climate, earthquakes, tsunamis, and other
cosmic events such as comet or meteoric collisions be explained? These
events would have to be part of a larger reality that lies beyond the
vision of human beings and even that of the gods.

WEAVING REALITY

Based on an etymological examination of their names, author Paul
C. Bauschatz suggests that the Norns' individual roles are aspects of one

task, with Urðr reflecting actions that are full, clear, and observable—in other words, actions that have come to fruition and are accomplished. Verðandi may be seen as the process that produces what Urðr completes. It is as if Verðandi is the mechanism or active principle of Urðr's creativity. As Skuld is involved with necessary or obligatory action—that which must become—she is different from the other two Norns.[3]

While I agree that their tasks seem to flow from one to the next, I believe that Bauschatz may have misinterpreted the direction of their actions. With this in mind, Urðr may be seen as the moment of manifestation—when a quantum vibration becomes physical matter. Verðandi is the progression or unfolding of that matter's existence, and Skuld represents the structures or requirements that define the course of that progression. From this perspective, the last few lines of this section of the *Völuspá,* "Þær lög lögðu, þær líf kuru alda börnum, ørlög seggja" would be better translated as, "Layers of reality they brought forth, describing the cycles of Time and speaking the primal patterns of the Cosmos."*

Scholars suggest that the line of the *Völuspá,* "skáru á skíði" ("on the wood they scored") refers to carving runes. This is one way to suggest that the Norns transform intangible energies into the physical reality in the same way the vibrations of speech are captured in a written alphabet. However, since our ancestors saw the world in terms of cycles, the flow of the Norns' creative energies were most likely circular or multidirectional. They have an ability to continuously manifest and unravel the nature of our reality.† In that interpretation, the "wood" they score may actually be referring to the Tree of Life, Yggdrasil. This would be a perfect metaphor for how Life is always being rewritten or remolded into new forms.

---

*This translation of "Þær lög lögðu, þær líf kuru alda börnum, ørlög seggja" is far closer to the intent of the Old Norse as described by Bauschatz and by Ralph Metzner in his book *The Well of Remembrance.*

†I believe that this idea is reflected in the way runic messages were inscribed. They were sometimes written left to right, other times right to left, and occasionally by having each line of writing alternate directions.

THE THREE MAY BE ONE

Among the Norns, Urðr appears to hold a more prominent place. It is she who is spoken about most often in Norse/Germanic mythic texts. Her name is the same as the word used to describe the action of the Norns. Urðr is also referred to as *Urð*. The word *Urð* or *Urðr* in Old Norse, *wyrd* in Old English and *wurd* in Old Saxon all have a common etymological origin. The Proto-Indo-European root word is *wert,* which means "to turn, rotate." It is she who is the cycle that takes the quantum vibrations of all possibility and transforms them into reality. In other words, anything that was or will be is under Urð's domain.

A WELLSPRING OF WISDOM

Urð also gives her name to the place where the Norns reside. Urðarbrunnr lies at the base of the World Tree. The Old Norse word *brunnur,* meaning "spring, well, or fountain," may have its root in the Proto-Indo-European word *bhreue* which means "to boil, bubble, effervesce, or burn."[4] Another Old Norse word, *kelda,* is also a feminine noun with some similar meanings. Along with describing a spring, bog, fountain, ice hole, and source, it also refers to the fontanelle or opening in the skull of an infant's head. This certainly could have parallels to the rush of water that precedes a child's crown emerging from his mother's womb.

In terms of Urðarbrunnr, it is the source for the water that gives eternal life to the forever green Yggdrasil. Every day, the tree is watered from the well. Since all realms are held in the World Tree's roots, trunk, and branches, the Norn and her fruitful well sustain the realms of the gods, the spirits, and humans. Everything depends on Urðarbrunnr, just as all possible realities spring forth from Urð's actions.

The twelfth-century chronicler of Icelandic folk stories, Snorri Sturluson suggests that there are actually three wells at the base of the tree. These are Urðarbrunnr, Hveergelmir (which means "bubbling,

Figure 6.1. Urð, the eldest and
most prominent Norn.

boiling spring" in Old Norse), and Mímisbrunnr (the well of the giant
Mimir, "the rememberer" or "wise one"). This peculiar circumstance is
most likely an error in Snorri's understanding of the old stories, which
were already centuries old by the time of his writing. It is more likely
that there is only one source and that it is the bubbling well of memory
and wisdom—the ultimate sacred creative vessel.[5]

In the far north, bodies of water were regarded as a gateway
between worlds. Such places were thought of as entrances into the
world of the spirits well into the Iron Age. Springs and wells were

thought to possess magical properties such as healing. This isn't surprising, as a spring bursting forth from a hillside or bubbling up in a pool provides a continuous supply of essential freshwater—free from disease-causing organisms.

This idea of a sacred well, pool, spring, or cauldron has parallels in other Northern European traditions. Among the Celtic tribes, the goddess Ceridwen has a cauldron of inspiration in which she brews the transformative elixir that will eventually create the great bard Taliesin. The Welsh giants Cymydei Cymeinfoll and her husband Llasar Llaes Gyfnewid owned the magical cauldron, Pair Dadeni. When the dead were placed inside this vessel they were born again into the world of the living.

In giving the Norn and her well so prominent a position, we can see parallels to the older, Paleolithic reverence of the feminine. Urð and her womblike well, function much like an archetypal Mother Goddess—the deep, watery mystery responsible for Life's continuity.

Our ancestors also perceived that water sources were places to perform divination and to contact the divine. Since Urð's well is the source of all wisdom, it is the ultimate repository of that which is sought by a shaman. The shaman enters the numinous world of wisdom to support and nurture the world of the living. This role puts the shaman in alignment with the Norn's action of continuance.

URÐ AND THE NEW PHYSICS

The New Physics suggests that the quantum vacuum or quantum plenum from which everything arises is a field of infinite possibility. It is the source of everything that has existed, that does exist, and that will exist.[6] Furthermore, this field of all potential from which matter arises is also described as a kind of light. This field of light is not only more fundamental than matter, it also supersedes space and time. Of course, this is not simply the familiar light of the electromagnetic spectrum but what another physicist, Mark Comings, Ph.D., refers to as

Figure 6.2. Urð's well, Urðarbrunnr, represents the primordial,
nurturing wellspring of all life.

a primordial, unifying "Sea of Radiance," in which everything exists.
Indeed, Comings suggests that all matter—everything that we understand as physical—is actually a kind of crystalized or condensed light.[7]

The primordial light that encompasses All That Is makes the shift
from formlessness into matter because of the "light" of consciousness. In stating this, physicists are not referring to ordinary, everyday
consciousness, but rather the higher, expanded consciousness human
beings access through the disciplines of meditation and the shamanic
state of awareness. Indeed, Comings suggests that human beings are
"hyper-dimensional crystal lattice" within the quantum plenum, with
an "indwelling light of consciousness." This description reveals the

spiritual nature of higher consciousness, in that this aspect of our nature is both the light of All That Is and the action that is continually creating matter. In other words, light and consciousness are inextricably interwoven and human consciousness is an intrinsic feature of the field of reality that has a critical role in not only physics but also the biology of all living beings.

Since Urð functions as this action of transforming potential into reality, it would suggest that Urð is a representation of the Divine Mind manifesting physical existence—the moment when spirit comes into form. Her sisters then equate to how consciousness continually reshapes our existence over the course of our life. Our levels of awareness restrain the forms of this continuous reshaping. If we function from the limited beliefs created by our sensory experiences of reality, we are not in higher awareness and so are more limited in our ability to intentionally shape our reality. Perceiving our pivotal role in cocreation and developing it to the fullest is only possible through stepping into an expanded state of awareness.

FREYJA SHOWS US THE WAY

Within this understanding of Urð, the Earth Goddess Freyja can be seen as a representation of fully conscious nature. It is only she who is able to glimpse what the Norns are weaving. Her ability to perceive the moment of Light being made manifest or "crystalizing" is what makes her the goddess of prophesy. By being able to "see" that which is normally hidden, or which lies beyond our ordinary experience of consciousness, she perceives the inner workings of reality. She is the self-aware being—embodying the "indwelling light of conscious-ness." Her ability to grasp the workings of All That Is positions her as the ultimate role model for any person who chooses to understand the nature of reality through the doorway of her or his own higher consciousness/spirit. In this way, she is guiding us to follow her aware-ness of the creative role of consciousness in manifesting our world.

This suggests that she represents a preserved memory of the archetypical mother of all shamans.

Like Freyja, all shamans have the ability to glimpse the moment when the formless energy of spirit enters the physical realm. Across cultures, shamanic rituals are designed to influence this mechanism by either bringing in beneficial energies from the realm of spirit or banishing energies that negatively impact the living. The understanding that every thing and being has a basis in the nonphysical word is a common thread in shamanism.

That point between formless and matter is the fulcrum on which creation depends. It is the process that is continually making and remaking our reality, and it is Urð's domain.

◆ Journeying to Urð— The Moment of Manifestation

The primordial giantess, Urð represents the precise moment when the primordial energy of the quantum plenum becomes tangible, physical matter. She is the alchemical creative moment when the light of spirit takes the form. Knowing Urð can assist us to better understand how our consciousness participates in what is materializing from her well.

This journey will be with your power animal to Urð. You will be going with your power animal and shamanic ancestor to be in the presence of this primordial force as giantess.

You may use the fire or a rattle or drum to make these journeys. If neither of those options is possible, by all means feel empowered to journey with a shamanic drumming recording that includes a callback signal.

For this exercise, you will need:

- Your rattle or drum or a recording of shamanic journey drumming
- Offering materials
- Some of your favorite food

- ◆ Your journal or a notebook and pen
- ◆ Fire-making supplies if you plan to use the fire to support your journey

◈ Making the Journey

1. Choose a time when you will be able to spend a long, uninterrupted time with the spirits.
2. Prepare yourself and all the materials as you did in the previous exercises. Once preparations are complete, honor the spirits of all directions, and ask them to bless the area where you will be working.
3. Now call your power animal to you, and merge with the animal. This spirit will protect your spirit body on your journey.
4. Next you will make an offering to the spirits of your ancestors as a part of maintaining reverent participatory relationships with them.

   As you did before, make your offering outdoors even if you are going to be journeying inside. Begin to rattle or drum softly for a few minutes or start the recording of shamanic journey drumming. At the beginning of the journey, imagine the incredibly long line of shamanic ancestors standing behind you. Notice how they are supporting you in this journey. Thank them in advance for their assistance in working with you by making your offering. Take a small bit of your favorite food and place it on the ground. Eat a small bit of this same food yourself in communion with them.
5. Once you have made your offerings and preparations, begin your journey.
6. Hold a strong intention to again meet with your shamanic ancestor. Keeping this intention, honor the spirits with your song.
7. When you meet your shamanic ancestor, greet her and ask her to take you to Urðarbrunnr at the base of Yggdrasil to meet the oldest Norn, Urð.
8. When you get to the well, ask your shamanic ancestor to guide you about how to proceed. On your first journey to this place you may only be able to watch Urð from a distance. Follow the loving guidance of your ancestral shaman.

9. Learn whatever you can during the experience. Again, allow your shamanic ancestor to guide the process. Receive the wisdom of the journey in whatever form you are given.

10. When you feel complete, be sure to thank your power animal, your shamanic ancestor, and Urð if you have been fortunate to interact with her. Return fully to ordinary consciousness. Once you feel fully back from your journey, make another offering to the ancestors and your shamanic helpers for their loving assistance.

Take the time to write down your experience with Urð. You may have a very clear idea of what you learned or you may have to sit with the experience for a while to understand all that you were given. Allow your heart to receive the gifts.

◈ Other Journey Explorations

- Journey with your shamanic ancestor and your power animal to ask them to take you to Urð's well again. Once in her presence, ask your shamanic ancestor how you may begin learning from being in Urð's presence. Repeat this at least monthly for a full year or until your shamanic ancestor feels that the work is complete.

- Journey to a teacher or power animal to ask, "What is the most important thing I gained from being at Urð's well?" Record the content of your journey and your perceptions about what you received.

- Journey to your shamanic ancestor: "How did you honor Urð, or what Urð represents?"

- What did you learn about manifestation from being close to Urð?

After each journey, thank your power animal, your teacher, your shamanic ancestor, and whatever other spirits you meet. Then make an offering outdoors to all the helping spirits.

◈ **Process Questions**

- ◆ Write down in your journal what it was like to be at the base of the World Tree, Yggdrasil, at Urð's well. Write down all that you felt.
- ◆ How has your experience with Urð begun to shift your perceptions about the nature of reality?
- ◆ What do you now think about your role in manifesting the physical realm? Write down all of your feelings, thoughts, and sensations.

7

Ørlög and Wyrd

Creation Has No Beginning or End

The Norse described two powerful forces that define and shape our existence. These are *Ørlög* and *Wyrd*.

The Norse concept of Ørlög has been described as a primordial law or template for reality. It has been described in terms of absolute structure onto which a life is written. This has been translated over the years as fate or the irreducible fundamental structure/law of reality that cannot be changed. It is also sometimes described as part of our legacy passed to us by our ancestors—a kind of genetic karma.

Wyrd is described as how the life is shaped within the predetermined framework of the Ørlög. It is how all of life unfolds within the Ørlög, and on a personal level it is a process of choice and evolution. If we think about these in terms of a card game, the commonly accepted characterization of Wyrd is how we are able to play the hand that our Ørlög deals us.

My sense is these common interpretations of Ørlög and Wyrd are far too limited. While they describe a portion of the interplay between such things as nature and nurture or genetics and epigenetics, they seem to be too stuck in an ordinary reality experience. It is my belief that somewhere along the process of passing centuries, these ideas about the fundamental nature of existence were inadvertently reduced to simplistic definitions that do not describe the original visionary perspective of the concepts.

In the context afforded us through the shamanic journey and echoed by the New Physics, we can better describe Ørlög as the quantum plenum, the playing field of infinite possibilities—as it is perceived through our awareness. In other words, our ability to create our existence from that infinite sphere is determined by our level of consciousness. This facility is affected by our perceptions and by the extent to which we have tapped into higher states of awareness.

According to Michael Talbot in his book *The Holographic Universe,* patterns of belief can become repeated so often that they become a "habit of nature." While we may come to accept any aspect of our consensual reality as an absolute truth, the fact is that these are only one of many possible manifestations of reality.

Within this context, Wyrd may be defined as the action of working with the threads of our own consciousness—our perceptions—to transform how we are able to manifest our life and our world. When seen through this lens, Ørlög is infinitely mutable and moldable through the working of Wyrd. To accomplish this, we need to realign ourselves with the way of being that our most ancient shamanic ancestors experienced and explored.

Working the Wyrd with intention involves a personal transformation. First, we need to become facile with expanding our awareness. This is accomplished through both meditation and the shamanic journey process. In either case, we have the experience of a deep opening up. Our perceptions of the nature of reality expand to include new perspectives, and we undergo a shift in our understanding of who we are and where we fit into the larger landscape of the cosmos. These changes are not secondhand teachings from Earthly teachers, but first-person experiences that not only inform our awake mind but also our subconscious mind as well as our physical, sensory, and emotional bodies. Having firsthand, personal visionary experiences transforms us on every level.

Refining how we work with our feelings is another aspect of intentionally affecting the Ørlög. It is for this reason that I have devoted

Figure 7.1. The Web of Wyrd represents all the shapes that can be expressed in the runes and so encompasses the innumerable ways we can shape the infinite possibilities of Ørlög into our tangible reality.

a great deal of one of my earlier books, *Spirit Walking: A Course in Shamanic Power,* to this subject. To be an effective cocreator, we need to align ourselves with the energies that are conducive to creating beauty, harmony, and health. This is because our consciousness is an amalgamation of our thoughts and feelings. Of the two, it is becoming clear that our feelings, and their intimate connection to our subconscious beliefs, have a greater impact on the unifying field of radiance than our conscious thoughts. Our feelings change our experience of daily life, they affect the expression of our DNA, and since they are nonlocal in nature they impact all other living beings across time and space.

Fostering deep feelings of love, gratitude, compassion, and appreciation can assist in this work. In addition, rooting out our fears and healing them is critical to changing our emotional landscape. This is necessary, as fear is a disruptive vibration that is contrary to the energies of creation. Fear wears many masks. It can be expressed as anxiety, anger, judgment, impatience, envy, jealousy, blame, shame, bitterness, feeling either inferior or superior to others, cowardice, or suspicion or can take other forms.

The way to begin rooting out our fears is by developing a compassionate observer self. Having that perspective can provide a vantage point through which we can look at our own behavior for clues to identifying our underlying fears. We can begin to ask ourselves questions about why we react a certain way, think certain thoughts, or follow certain patterns of behavior. Once we identify the ways fear is affecting our life, we can choose to find out the source of the fear and heal it at the root. In so doing, we not only transform our inner landscape and the space around us, we contribute to healing the collective.

This leads me to share the third transformation we need to make; that is, to begin looking at the bigger picture and paying attention to how our actions affect the world. We are "entangled" on the quantum level. As parts of our Earthly ecosystem, we are interdependent with all other beings. Our spirits are aspects of a whole intelligence—a larger consciousness that holds all of the wisdom that ever was or will be. We humans can no longer afford to live our lives as though we exist in an isolated bubble. Everything we do, feel, and think affects the web of Life. Our connectedness is an absolute truth, as no thing or being can ever be separate from All That Is.

◆ Journeying to Better Understand Ørlög and Wyrd

To get a better understanding of Ørlög and Wyrd, it is important to have first-person experiences. These concepts are not rooted in our sensory experience of the world. Therefore, experiencing them in an expanded awareness state can inform us on levels beneath ordinary consciousness. When we journey we take along our emotional body, our subconscious experience, our sensory awareness, and our spiritual body. This gives us the opportunity to input information, healing, guidance, and insight into several of our channels at once! Having a felt experience helps us to "know" even before our conscious mind can understand.

The purpose of these journeys is to have your power animal and shamanic ancestor give you experiences of the Ørlög and Wyrd. These are best done as three separate journeys.

1. For your first journey, have your spirits give you an experience of the Ørlög.
2. As a second journey, have your spirits give you an experience of Wyrd.
3. For a third journey, ask to have an experience of how the Ørlög and Wyrd interact.

You may use the fire or a rattle or drum to make these journeys. If neither of those options is possible, by all means feel empowered to journey with a shamanic drumming recording that includes a callback signal.

For each journey exercise, you will need:

- Your rattle or drum or a recording of shamanic journey drumming
- Offering materials
- Some of your favorite food
- Your journal or a notebook and pen
- Fire-making supplies if you plan to use the fire to support your journey

◈ Making the Journey

1. Choose a time when you will be able to spend a long, uninterrupted time with the spirits.

2. Prepare yourself and all the materials as you did in the previous exercises. Once preparations are complete, honor the spirits of all directions, and ask them to bless the area where you will be working.

3. Now call your power animal to you, and merge with the animal. This spirit will protect your spirit body on your journey.

4. Next you will make an offering to the spirits of your ancestors as a part of maintaining reverent participatory relationships with them.

   As you did before, make your offering outdoors even if you are going to be journeying inside. Begin to rattle or drum softly for a few minutes or start the recording of shamanic journey drumming. At the beginning of the journey, imagine the incredibly long line of shamanic ancestors standing behind you. Notice how they are supporting you in this journey. Thank them in advance for their assistance in working with you by making your offering. Take a small bit of your favorite food and place it on the ground. Eat a small bit of this same food yourself in communion with them.

5. Once you have made your offerings and preparations, begin your journey.

6. Hold a strong intention to again meet with your shamanic ancestor. Keeping this intention, honor the spirits with your song.

7. When you meet your shamanic ancestor, greet him and ask him to take you to experience the first journey.

8. When you get to the well, ask your shamanic ancestor to guide you about how to proceed.

9. Learn whatever you can during the experience. Again, allow your shamanic ancestor to guide the process. Receive the wisdom of the journey in whatever form you are given.

10. When you feel complete, be sure to thank your power animal, your shamanic ancestor, and any other spirits you have been fortunate to interact with. Return fully to ordinary consciousness. Once you feel fully back from your journey, make another offering to the ancestors and your shamanic helpers for their loving assistance.

    You may have a very clear idea of what you learned or you may have to sit with the experience for a while to understand what you were given. Allow your heart to receive the gifts.

11. Repeat this format for each of the journeys.

◈ Other Journey Explorations

Working the Wyrd with intention involves a personal transformation. The following journeys can support you to shift your perceptions and work more effectively with the Wyrd. There are three categories of journeys: those about awareness, journeys about working with feelings, and those about understanding how to work in harmony with all the realms of existence. In each case, journey with your shamanic ancestor and your power animal.

JOURNEYS ABOUT AWARENESS

- Journey to teacher, power animal, or your shamanic ancestor to ask, "What is the true nature of consciousness?" Record the content of your journey and your perceptions about what you received.
- Journey to teacher, power animal, or your shamanic ancestor to ask, "What is the true nature of reality?" As you did before, record the content of your journey and your perceptions about what you received.

JOURNEYS ABOUT FEELINGS

- Journey to teacher, power animal, or your shamanic ancestor to ask, "How is my life a product of my perceptions?"
- Journey to teacher, power animal, or your shamanic ancestor to ask to meet an aspect of yourself that will be your compassionate observer.
- Journey to meet with your "compassionate observer self" to learn how your unconscious fears motivate your behaviors.
- Journey to teacher, power animal, or your shamanic ancestor to ask, "How can my unconscious fears be healed?"

- Journey to teacher, power animal, or your shamanic ancestor to ask, "How can I develop a life of gratitude and love?"

**JOURNEYS ABOUT WORKING IN HARMONY
WITH ALL THAT IS**

- Journey to teacher, power animal, or your shamanic ancestor to ask, "How do my feelings affect All That Is?"
- Journey to teacher, power animal, or your shamanic ancestor to ask, "How can I live my life so that it benefits All That Is?"

After each journey, thank your power animal, your teacher, your shamanic ancestor, and whatever other spirits you meet. Then make an offering outdoors to all the helping spirits.

◈ **Process Questions**

- Write down in your journal what it was like to discover the relationship between Ørlög and Wyrd. Write down all that you felt.
- How has learning about how you affect All That Is impacted your shamanic path?
- What steps are you taking to transform your way of being so that you produce more harmony?

8

Seiðr as Shamanic Ritual

Shamans have always functioned as intermediaries between our ordinary human world and other beings. These could include the denizens of nature as well as the many other spirits. This work was accomplished by traveling between these worlds in a state of trance. A shaman's work benefits the human community while keeping harmony with the environment, the ancestors, and other beings. It is humankind's oldest spiritual tradition.

Even though European Eurasia experienced many waves of immigrants during prehistory, the threads of this earliest way of relating to spirit persisted in northern Scandinavia. Agriculture was slow to spread into the region as the more ancient way of living through hunting and gathering remained a viable survival solution for far longer than in the south. Due to this, the older ways of knowing the world connected to that lifestyle persisted as well. Remnants of shamanic spirituality survived in the folk traditions of the Scandinavians because the inhabitants lived at the northern fringes of Europe. Yet while places like Siberia, Central Asia, and the Arctic preserved intact shamanic culture up to the twentieth century, Christianity finally displaced most of the shamanic practices in northern Scandinavia during the late period of the Viking Age.* Because the Icelanders wrote down the Norse mythic

---

*The Sami people of the Scandinavian Arctic retained their shamanic culture until the Christian church's organized persecution of them in the seventeenth and eighteenth centuries.

stories and traditions, we have many more clues about what the ancient European shaman's world might have been like, especially when examined in conjunction with other shamanic cultures in northern Eurasia, such as the Sami and the tribes of Siberia.

One practice that was fairly well documented in the Icelandic sagas is *seiðr*. The Icelandic sagas, written down in the twelfth to fourteenth centuries, have been given more credence by archaeological finds such as the Oseberg ship burial. This Viking longboat was buried under a large mound in the year 834 CE in Vestfold, Norway. Buried inside were two women, one in her fifties and the other in her seventies, who were surrounded by lavish grave goods. Their high-status burial accoutrements included unusual ritual objects such as staffs with iron rattle heads, which made it clear that these women were not royalty, as early twentieth-century investigators once thought. These women were Viking Age shamans. Women in ancient Norse society were the ones who primarily practiced shamanism or seiðr. A woman who practiced with art was known as a *seiðkona* or *völva*.[1] (A note here, some men also practiced this art of seeing and were titled *seiðmaðr;* since seiðr was commonly practiced by women, I will use female pronouns and feminine descriptive words more often. The masculine aspect of this work will be discussed in greater length in the chapter pertaining to Oðinn.)

A line from the short *Völuspá* of the *Hyndluljóð* saga reads, *"Eru völur allar frá Viðlólfi,"* which translates to, "All völur come from Viðólfur," a name that has been translated as "tree wolf." However, some researchers have suggested that the word *Viðólfur* should actually be *Viðólfu,* which would make the line read, "All völur come from the first one—the one from the Tree."[2] If this is correct in her premise, then Yggdrasil, the foundation of all Life, and Freyja are interwoven. Since the World Tree is a very common way that shamans travel between the realms, this suggestion is yet another allusion to Freyja's role as the First Shaman. In this way, all völur (plural of völva) whether women or men were following in her footsteps. They were the shamans of their culture.

WISE WOMEN

During the Viking Age, practitioners of seiðr were often described as women past their childbearing years. This image of a magical woman has parallels to the ancient figures of matronly females I described in an earlier chapter. These women also did not carry clan or lineage names.[3] Unlike other women of their time, they were not identified as "belonging" to a father or chieftain. They had a unique position in society and operated outside the ordinary way of life.

Even without the typical affiliations of family or clan, völur were high-status women. This is clear from the wealth and rich adornments that accompanied them on their final journey to the other world. The Oseberg ship in which the two seiðkonas or völur were interred was fitted with a silver inlayed stern and, in spite of being raided for treasure prior to being uncovered by archaeologists in 1903, still contained finely crafted objects, luxurious clothing, tapestries, and other expensive goods. Indeed, Scandinavian archaeologists have found over forty high-status women's graves containing these kinds of lavish contents.

The graves also held ritual paraphernalia. Like their Paleolithic and Neolithic sisters, these women carried the tools of their trade into death. Various charms such as keys, small statues, and animal bones, teeth, or claws were often found in burials of völur. A völva buried in Fyrkat, Denmark, was buried with a box containing her talismans, or *taufr*. These included an owl pellet, small bones from birds and animals, as well as henbane seeds. When thrown on a fire, henbane seeds can produce a hallucinogenic smoke that gives those who inhale it a sense of flying, which may have enhanced the völva's trance.[4] The völur who were buried in the Oseberg ship were similarly outfitted with a pouch of cannabis seeds for their journey beyond life.

Völur were also buried with a staff, not only a shamanic implement but also an insignia of their profession. The Old Norse term *völva* has been widely translated to mean a woman "wand carrier" or "magical staff bearer." Many shamans use a ceremonial staff as an object of

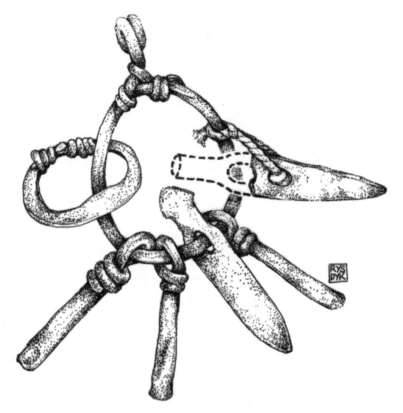

Figure 8.1. This silver amulet ring, which includes three staffs, a sword, a spearhead (incomplete), and a fire striker, was found in Klinta, Köpings parish, Öland, Sweden. Rings of charms like this one have been found across the Viking world in association with female burials and may have been a part of völur "tool kits."

spiritual power. Held during the visionary ritual of seiðr, these *seiðstafr*, or *völ*, may have been representations of the World Tree. This symbolic reference is common among shamans from the Arctic to Asia and down to the Peruvian Amazon.[5] Since the spiritual principle uniting the spirit worlds for the Norse was the Great Tree, Yggdrasil, it makes sense that völur would carry a staff. Being able to travel into the realms of the spirits is a critical requirement for any shamanic practitioner. Knowing the way around the realms to contact the spirits who lived in them would be an essential aspect of being able to negotiate harmony, gain insight, or access much needed wisdom. The wand or staff would function as a connection to all the realms of spirit as well as another kind of tether to help a völva return to this world.

In addition to the obvious connection to the World Tree that unites the realms of spirit, a *seiðworker's* staff also has parallels to a spinner's distaff. A distaff is a device that holds combed fibers that are ready to be spun into yarn or thread. When one is using a hand drop spindle, a distaff about a meter long is held upright in the crook of the arm on the opposite side of the body as the hand holding the spindle. From that position, the fleece or other loose fibers are pulled a bit at a time onto the twirling spindle. This action literally spins the fuzzy filaments into a smooth, usable thread or yarn that can be either knitted or woven into cloth for making garments. Several surviving examples of seiðstafr that were found in burials are iron and brass representations of these kinds of distaffs. Far too heavy to be used for the spinning of fibers, these staffs were clearly used for another purpose.

Taller distaffs are held between a spinner's knees and function in the same manner. These distaffs can also have a dual function. Spun yarn or thread can be loaded onto the tall distaff so that it functions as a spool. From there the yarn can be threaded onto a standing loom. These taller distaffs are of a length that could be used for a hiking stick and may have inspired longer seiðstafr.* Whether tall or short, distaffs literally hold the potential for what will eventually be spun or woven.

A woman's grave excavated in Köpingsvik on the island of Öland in Sweden held a cache of a seiðkona's or völva's ritual tools. Interred in a ship amidst several animal sacrifices and goods from as far away as Persia, this woman was buried with an iron and bronze staff that is just a few centimeters short of a meter long. Iron staffs are used by shamans among tribes like the Enets of Siberia,[6] as are iron representations of ordinary objects and images of birds and animals. All of these are used as a part of shamanic rituals. The völva's staffs found in several burials

---

*Reconstructions of a Viking-era warp-weighted floor loom suggest that a staff at least 2 meters tall would have been rested on the side of the loom.

resemble ceremonial versions of the distaff used for spinning flax or wool. Along with the burial at Öland, examples of these metal staffs have been uncovered in Gävle, Sweden, and from a grave at Fuldby, near Ringsted in Denmark.[7] Since it is iron, it would have been far too heavy for ordinary purposes. For this reason, the metal staffs were most likely ritual objects—seiðstafr used for spinning magic in the spiritual realms. The Oseberg völva was buried with both an iron staff and a longer birch staff that had been split and then hollowed out and glued. The later staff may have been used as a flute or to "shoot" magic via the völva's breath, as one might do with a blowgun.

Spinning is one way of representing the work of the Norns. The action of taking formless fluff and spinning it into usable thread is a marvelous metaphor for Urð's role in transforming formless potential into physical reality. It is a magical act of creation. Indeed, the word *seiðr* has some relation to making various forms of cordage. While the etymology of *seiðr* is unclear, related words in other Germanic languages are related to cord, string, snare, or halter.[8] That would certainly relate to the metaphor for spinning threads of reality. Since the völva also sang and spoke her journey, we could also say she was "spinning a tale" of her interactions with the spirits.

SONGS FOR THE SPIRITS

This reference to using the voice is quite apt as the Old Norse seer would alter consciousness by the use of ecstatic chanting of *varðlokur*. After the songs brought the völva into a visionary trance state, she would begin speaking prophecy. In the Icelandic sagas, the words spoken by the seer have a poetic or skaldic quality. Such is often the case when the spirits speak though a shaman. The ordinary way of speaking is shifted into poetic language often rich with evocative imagery.*

While no records of original varðlokur songs were preserved,

---

*The book, *Old Norse Women's Poetry: The Voices of Female Skalds* by Sandra Ballif Straubhaar is filled wonderful examples of völur prophecies and other women's poetry.

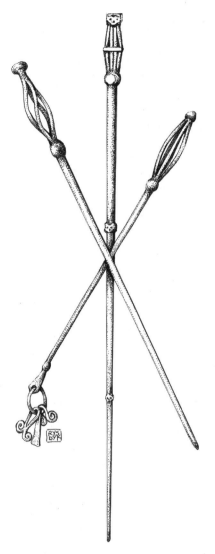

Figure 8.2. Iron staffs like these examples have been unearthed all across Scandinavia. These and other wood and mixed metal examples are associated with high-status burials of women and more infrequently of men.

they were most likely repetitive, singsong melodies that supported the expansion of consciousness. Any repetitive stimulus can contribute to attaining an altered state and trance. The brain entrains itself to repetitive stimuli such as pulsing lights, dancing, drumming, rattling, and chanting. One who has been trained and has practiced working with this alteration of consciousness can use supportive stimuli such as these to intentionally shift into a visionary state. Since much of the völva's vocation had metaphoric parallels to the practices of spinning and weaving, it is easy to see the varðlokur songs in this light. The songs would have been used to "spin" the threads of shamanic reality for the seiðkona and to direct the weave of her ritual work.

Other purposes of the varðlokur may be found by exploring the etymology of the word. The first section, "varð," is related to the Old Norse word vǫrð, which is often thought to mean "watch/watcher/watching" and also "to guard." However it may also be related to varða, which has several meanings, such as "to happen," "to come to pass," and "to answer for/to," or "belonging to." The second half of the word may be related to the Old Norse word for coaxing, luring, or enticing, also meaning "to bolt or unbolt a door." Combining these two parts, varðlokur may be seen as shamanic songs that call the spirits, offer protection (either through the songs themselves or through the protective spirits they call), support a völva in entering and maintaining her trance, assist in divining future events, and open or close the gates of nonordinary reality.

Since the seeresses of the sagas seem to have traveled widely to perform seiðr, a chorus of local women and girls in each area usually sang the protective and trance-inducing varðlokur songs. This means that the songs themselves were an important aspect of the cultural tradition. Perhaps varðlokur songs were magical variations of more common songs. These melodies may have been similar to songs used to accompany rhythmically repetitive activities such as spinning or weaving.

During the Viking Age, the people would have lived on large farms spread around the island, with most of them only a short distance from the coast. During the time the sagas were written, Iceland's population is believed to have varied between 40,000 and 60,000 people during the tenth to fourteenth centuries.[9] Even though the current population is roughly six times that number, it is still quite sparsely populated save for the city of Reykjavik.* For rural women and girls to know these songs all across the island, they had to have been passed from mother to

---

*I personally witnessed this during my 2005 tour around the island nation.

daughter and practiced often, so that they were easily recalled when a traveling völva required them to be sung. Yet Erik the Red's Greenland saga suggests by the time Christianity was prevalent singers were in shorter supply. When Þórbjörg lítilvölva (Thorbjorg, the Little Völva) was summoned to provide aid during a famine, she required a singer to sing for her. Since by that time Greenland had been Christianized, no one at that farm still knew the songs. A young woman was summoned who was named Guðriður. She said that when she was in Iceland her foster-mother Halldis taught her the songs. While she was very reluctant to sing the seiðr chants, as she was a Christian, she was convinced by the headman of the district to sing for the ceremony. She sang the varðlokur songs so well and beautifully that those present were sure they had never heard more lovely singing. The seiðkona thanked her for the song, stating, "Many spirits are now present, which were charmed to hear the singing. They had previously shunned us and would grant us no obedience. And now many things stand revealed, which before were hidden both from me and from others."[10]

Singing, or the use of song to enter or maintain trance, is common to many shamanic cultures. One of my teachers, the Nepalese jhankri Bhola Banstola, depends on singing as well as drumming to alter consciousness and sustain the shamanic trance. The same is true for other Eurasian shamans with whom I have studied. The late Ulchi Grandfather Mikhail "Misha" Duvan and Tuvan shaman Ai-Churek both used their voices as integral aspects of their shamanic practice.

The Icelandic *Völuspá* mentions one seeress named Heiður who traveled around with a *raddlið*, her personal chorus of fifteen young men and fifteen young women. Since other seiðkonas who are mentioned in the sagas do not have this kind of entourage she must have been either particularly revered for her skill or not an ordinary völva.[11] According to the writer Näsström, the jötunn (giantess) völur Heiður (also known as Gullveig or "gold[en] power" in a female form) is most likely referring to Freyja, herself, and so reinforces the idea that this goddess is the Norse version of the mother of all shamans.[12]

Norse shamans were also able to practice their art without a chorus. In those cases, other methods were employed. One method was *útiseta,* or "sitting out," which involved a time of introspection in nature to receive a vision or to perform divination. During this vision-questing ritual the völva would sit with her staff and sing in concert with the elements, animals, birds, and transcendent nature spirits that were called *landvættir.* These land wights or spirits of nature were thought to protect and promote the vitality of the places where they live and were a source of wisdom. Sitting out and immersing oneself in the world of nature to receive inspiration and wisdom may have provided the original seed for the völva's songs. The Finnish epic poem *The Kalevala* has a passage that speaks beautifully to this connection:

> *Many runes the cold has taught me,*
> *Many lays the rain has brought me,*
> *Other songs the winds have sung me.*
> *Many birds from many forests,*
> *Oft have sung me lays n concord*
> *Waves of sea, and ocean billows,*
> *Music from the many waters,*
> *Music from the whole creation,*
> *Oft have been my guide and master.*
> *~THE KALEVALA*[13]

The word *útiseta* is derived from a thirteenth-century Icelandic law that outlawed *"útiseta at vekja tröll upp ok fremja heiðni,"* which translates to, "the act of sitting out to provoke/wake up trolls and practice paganism"; in other words, those spiritual beliefs that lie outside the Christian paradigm.[14] This practice has many parallels to shamanic traditions of spending time isolated from other human beings in nature for the purpose of connecting with spiritual resources or to receive a vision. The spirit journey of the völva during her wilderness quest may have also taken the seer to Urð and the World Tree, Yggdrasil, to seek council.[15]

Ancestors might have been accessed in a similar way for wisdom. *"Sitja á haugi"* or "to sit on a barrow" involved performing útiseta on a burial mound or barrow. These burial mounds were thought to be the residence of the dead who were buried beneath them. The ancient Norse believed that people had multiple souls.* The animating principle was the aspect of the person that left with the final breath and was part of the fabric of the cosmos and so also a part of the gods and nature. The "free soul" or dream soul would be freed from the body during sleep or trance. The "conscious soul," which held the emotions and the will, was located in the physical body. That was only released when the body or *haugbui* was fully destroyed though immolation or complete decay. At that point the conscious soul was free to journey to the realm of the dead.[16] With this understanding of soul it is easier to understand why powerful ancestors may have been buried under the home turf. It would mean that their conscious soul could continue to be a resource for help, healing, protection, and divination. Offerings of food and drink were placed on burial mounds with the idea that the deceased would return the favor by caring for the land and people. To sit on such a barrow and enter trance would have given the seiðkona easy access to the wisdom of her ancestors along with the spirits of nature.

The ship in which the Oseberg shamans were buried was held fast to the earth with a large stone. This was clear evidence that the ship was not for sailing but instead it was anchored in a safe harbor.[17] Not only did this allow the women to continue to protect the homestead and its people, it also echoed the shamanic requirement of having a secure place from which to fly through the realms and return safely. Every visionary journey has a beginning and an end and is only effective if the spiritual seeker is able to fully return to impart the wisdom she or he has gleaned

---

*This multisoul concept is common throughout Siberia and Central Asia. Mongols believe the human soul has three parts, while some tribes believe that four and five soul aspects exist.

while with the spirits. Having a tether to this world makes the return after roaming the worlds much easier. In other words, the burial ship could have provided them a way to continue their shamanic journeys after death.

Another interpretation is that the völva's people were striving to keep her from "sailing away" so that she would remain available to continue serving her community. In this way, she would remain in her barrow forever where other shamans could continue to seek her counsel.

THE TRAPPINGS OF RITUAL OFFICE

The most detailed description of a Norse shaman's ritual costume can be found in the Saga of Erik the Red.[18] This is a thirteenth-century report of an event that occurred two centuries earlier. During that time there was severe famine in Greenland. Those who had gone out on hunting expeditions had found little success, and some had never returned.

Þórkel, the headman of Herjolfsness called for Þórbjörg lítilvölva. This "little völva" was the youngest of nine sister seers,* but she was the only one still alive. It was her custom in winter to attend feasts, and she was always invited. In preparation for her arrival, the headman's house was cleaned and prepared, as was the custom when such women were being received. A high seat was made ready for her with a cushion on it, which was stuffed with hen's feathers.

The seiðkona arrived in the evening with the man who had been sent to escort her. She wore an ankle-length blue or black cloak† fastened with straps and adorned with stones all the way down to the hem. She had a necklace of glass beads. On her head she wore a black lambskin hood lined with cat's fur. She carried her ritual distaff with a

---

*The late Tuvan shaman Ai-Churek was one of nine daughters of a mother who had eight other sisters, all of whom were shamans.

†In Örvar-Odd's Saga, the völva also wears a blue or black cloak and carries a similar distaff.

brassbound knob studded with stones. She wore a belt made of amadou felt, from which hung a large pouch in which she kept the charms she needed for her work.* On her feet were hairy calfskin shoes with long thick laces that had large metal buttons on the ends. She wore catskin gloves, with the fur inside, no doubt to honor one of Freyja's personal cat spirit helpers or fylgjur.

After introducing her to the gathering, Þórkel the headman took her by the hand and led her to the seat that had been prepared for her. She was provided with dishes prepared only for her. She had a porridge made of goat milk and a dish made of hearts from all the kinds of animals at the homestead. She ate from the dishes with a brass spoon and a knife with a walrus-tusk handle bound with two rings of copper. The blade of the knife had a broken point.

Ritual costume is an important aspect of many shamanic traditions, and all of the shamans I have been fortunate to study with have used ceremonial garments as a part of their work. The early twentieth-century anthropologist M. A. Czaplicka described Siberian shaman costumes in great detail in her 1914 book, *Aboriginal Siberia: A Study in Social Anthropology*. She observed that shamans looked like everyday people most of the time but that when they were engaging with spirits they wore special clothing and wielded special instruments.[19] These costumes usually have several important roles. They offer ritual significance and indicate when the shaman is no longer operating as an ordinary person. Ceremonial attire can offer protection for the shaman by way of charms that are painted, sewn, or tied to the costume. The attire can support the shaman in embodying her tutelary spirits. In these cases the costume may have some representation of the spirit or spirits that are being honored or embodied.

---

*This is interesting, as amadou, or touchwood, is the tinder fungus *Fomes fomentarius*. It is commonly used to start fires and stop bleeding. Although caps of this felt are still made in Romania, a belt of this substance would not have been very durable and so must have been specifically a ceremonial object. It may also been part of the seiðkona's fantastic appearance as the fungus felt also emits a glow as it decays.

The hood worn by the seiðkona was not only a simple covering for the head but also most likely used during the ceremony to isolate the seer from ordinary reality. Shamans often employ blindfolds or masks during their rituals, and the hood may have functioned in the same fashion. Seiðr workers are said to have "gone under the cloak" during rituals and while performing the útiseta, or vision-seeking ritual.

Ritual garb can also include specific tools that assist the shaman in her or his work. For the völva, the seiðstafr would certainly be such an object. A few völur employed drums during their sessions, like the neighboring Sami shamans or noaide;[20] however, more often other sound-making instruments were used. Along with their seiðstafr, the Oseberg women had five highly decorated, wooden posts topped with carved animal heads that held iron rattles with them on their final journey into the spirit realm. These rattle posts were also found with handles that would have allowed them to be carried or perhaps to attach them to a larger construction.[21]

Other rattles such as miniature seiðstafr, spearheads, and swords, keys, and other shapes were found strung on rings* that could have been either attached to the clothing or staff or held in the hand. Rattling metal objects could have added a further dimension to the repetitive stimulation used to produce trance. Iron jingles are common in Siberian shamanism and have been included as parts of the costume. Many tribes across Asia utilize noisy iron bustles worn around the waist, iron talismans sewn to the shaman's coat, and iron staffs with jingling rings. In keeping with that idea, several seiðkona burials included small metal chair amulets,[22] which are suggestive of the *seiðhjallr* or high seat, in which the völva sits for her work.

The völva who was buried in Köpingsvik on the island of Öland in Sweden was interred wearing a bear pelt. Like the Viking berserkers or "bear shirt" warriors who donned a bearskin to invoke the power of the bear, perhaps this woman also embodied the bear spirit. Her con-

---

*These rattling amulets were made from iron, bronze, and silver.

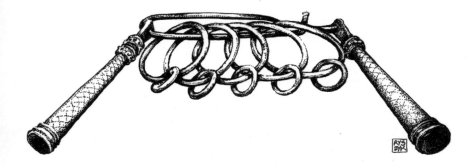

Figure 8.3. A decorated iron rattle found in the burial mound at Oseberg. It was found connected by rope to a carved wooden post topped with a dragon's head. Collection of the Viking Ship Museum, Museum of Cultural History of the University of Oslo.

nection to bears has parallels to Siberian as well as Sami shamanism, as these cultures also deified the bear. Indeed myths provide evidence for a circumpolar bear cult, and the Chavet cave reveals evidence of a cave bear ritual as far back as the Upper Paleolithic in Europe. It is clear that for our ancestors who lived in the north, the bear was a creature most worthy of veneration.

In his book *Man, God and Magic,* Ivar Lissner suggests that bears have been venerated by ancient people because they were thought to be in communication with the spirits of nature as well as those of the sky realms.[23] Among cultures that venerate the bear there is the sense that this animal is an archetypal messenger to the supernatural world. A bear enters the earth in the autumn and appears to die and yet while "dead" gives birth so she can resurrect to bring forth life in the spring. In this way, the bear, especially the she-bear, represents the one who lives between the worlds of life and death and of the worlds beneath and above the earth. Lissner also suggests that our prehistoric ancestors may have thought of the Bear Mother as the first mythopoetic universal mother of all life who predates all the other mother goddesses and madonnas of humankind.[24] Marija Gimbutas agrees that in the Old Europe of prehistory, creatures such as the bear, as well as the cat, the pig, the snake, the ram, the bull, and the bird are all associated with the primordial goddess of life, death, and regeneration.[25]

Perhaps the Köpingsvik völva's animal ally or personal spirit helper (fylgja) was the bear. Wearing a bearskin would have signified her connection to this spirit, and enrobing her would have echoed her ability to merge with that spirit in the same manner of Freyja's falcon-feathered cloak. *Hamskipti,* which is shape-shifting into an animal form, was another shamanistic aspect of seiðr. For coastal people this could have been either a sea mammal such as a walrus, whale, or seal or a powerful terrestrial animal or bird. Projecting the merged animal spirit form to another location was also possible and would have been accomplished through chanting or song, as the act was also referred to as *gandreið.*

THE HIGH SEAT

As I stated earlier, several völur burials included small metal chair amulets, which are suggestive of the seiðhjallr or high seat in which the völva sits for her work. The seiðkona is literally and figuratively set apart from others as she works. When performing her divinatory or oracular duties she is raised above others in an obvious metaphor for the way that her skills set her apart from other women. In addition, the high seat has ordinary reality parallels to the art of spinning. When spinning fibers into yarn or thread, the spindle must hang down below the spinner's arms. To accomplish this, a spinner often stands or sits in an elevated space so that the spindle can drop farther, thereby creating a larger quantity of yarn before having to stop to wind the result onto the spindle. A woman might sit or stand in the attic and allow the spindle to drop down to the floor below. In the modern Norwegian language, the attic of a home can be called a hjell or hjallr.[26]

Erik the Red's Greenland saga mentions the seiðhjallr as a platform built especially for the seiðr ritual. The oracular ceremony occurred at night, and the surrounding darkness must have made the scene even more powerful for those gathered below her. The literal manifestation

Figure 8.4. Silver charms representing chairs have been associated
with völur graves across the Viking world.

of the seer providing a higher wisdom would have become inescapable
in such a scene.

Interestingly, the Ulchi shamans of southeastern Siberia's Amur
River area performed a ceremony on a platform. The *kasaa* ritual
was a combination of both the shaman's oracular and psychopomp
duties—that is, offering spiritual wisdom, as well as guiding the spirits
of the dead to a safe place in the Lower World. When I studied with
Grandfather Misha, he performed this ceremony at twilight. During
this ritual, he stood on a platform that was supported by two trees. The
effect was of him standing in a gateway or doorway. From the platform
the spirits spoke through him to those of us assembled. The spirits
spoke messages and asked questions to those gathered below. Through
the ceremony, he trembled with spiritual power and gestured with his
arms. The powerful discourse with the spirits made clear who among us

would be chosen for healing during a later ceremony. At the same time, he guided the souls of those same people's loved ones who had never properly crossed over after death.

When Grandfather's helper spirits left his body after his work was completed, he collapsed like a marionette whose strings had been severed. He toppled off the platform into the arms of those who had been assigned the task of catching his ninety-four-year-old body. The effect on those of us gathered that evening was both deeply touching and awe inspiring.

Oðinn, the great Norse seeker god to whom Freyja taught seiðr, also has a high seat or throne. Lifting him above all others of the Æsir, the name of his throne Hliðskjálf translates to either "doorway-bench" or "watchtower."[27] This certainly would be a way to describe the perch the seiðkona uses to step into the realm of spirit. From this lofty seat, she was like Freyja, able to witness the weaving of reality being done by the Norns.

9

Seiðr and
the Sami Connection

Writing about the Old Norse shamanic practices would be incomplete if we didn't also look at the similarities with those other people with whom the Vikings shared the Scandinavian Peninsula.

The very first peoples entering the region entered from the south, migrating up as the ice sheets retreated farther north approximately 11,000 years ago. These Upper Paleolithic hunter-gatherers would have followed routes through Doggerland and up along the coastal areas of the southern part of the area. Recent genetic research has reinforced this model by finding that the genetic pool of modern male Norwegians is mainly composed of genes that were present in Europe as early as the Paleolithic period.

Subsequent waves of people entered the peninsula during the Mesolithic Age approximately 8,000 years ago. These people would have been groups that carried genes from groups of indigenous populations living in Central Europe and the Indo-Europeans who entered from the east. This correlates well with Marija Gimbutas's suggestions of the profound cultural mixing that occurred in Europe and that we see still echoed in Old Norse mythology. The telltale signs left in the genetic code prove again that despite the cultures being very different, these two groups found a way to coexist for the sake of survival.

A second incidence of cultural collision would have occurred a few thousand years later when the hunter-gatherer Sami people, who had arrived from the northeastern Arctic, migrated southward onto the peninsula.[1] This contact would have remained sporadic until the Iron Age, when people from the south began to drive traditional Sami culture northward, primarily through assimilation. This has been reinforced by Sami gravesites that show remains with Nordic and Baltic traits. This was accelerated during the height of the Viking Age migratory period and into the early Middle Ages. Trade occurred between the groups with Sami animal hides and furs being exchanged for salt, metal blades, and different kinds of coins that were used for ornamentation.

The Sami people are represented in Old Norse literature in the sagas recorded by the mid-thirteenth-century Icelandic writer Snorri Sturluson. They are portrayed as accomplished skiers, archers, and hunters who wear animal skins and furs, and certain Sami are represented as masters of sorcery. Some Sami were also known to be not only practitioners of witchcraft but also teachers of the magical arts.[2] Even though assimilation of the Sami occurred, there are still many examples of Sami people, and those who were part Sami, being referred to with derogatory and racist epithets. Interestingly, some of these derogatory descriptions or references to the Sami people were oddly otherworldly in nature. Some Sami represented in the Icelandic sagas were referred to as trolls, dwarves, and *bergrisi* or "hill giants." Trolls in Norse myths are ancient, wild, and untamed nature spirits associated with witchcraft. They live in small groups in out-of-the-way places such as caves, mountains, or isolated rocky areas. Dwarves are *svartálfar,* or "dark elves." They are magical, master craftsmen who live in an unseen subterranean realm.

Referring to the Sami as bergrisi, a form of jötunn or giant, is especially telling. As I wrote earlier in this book, the giants are seen throughout Norse mythology as primordial, wild beings that were present before the Norse gods. Since we now know that ancient Central Europeans made it to the area first, this suggests that the Sami people *represented* something older, mysterious, and frightening. They were hunters and gatherers, and the Old Norse people were farmers. When the Sami and Old Norse people made contact, I believe that the ancient trauma preserved in cultural memory—of the time when ancestors had met "strangers" in their world—was triggered again. It is why the wandering Sami are seen as mysterious, somewhat dangerous, and primordial in Norse literature. Unlike the Old Norse, the Sami weren't settled into farms. They roamed through the landscape and worked with the seasons, the patterns of ripening plants, and the migration of game. They were clothed in skins and furs, lived in portable tentlike dwellings, and left little in the way of hardscaping to show where they had been. For this reason the settled, agrarian, and pastoral Norse would have considered Sami land as uninhabited and would have been consistently surprised by Sami wanderers appearing "out of nowhere." Indeed, traditional Sami territories would have substantially overlapped the Viking world so their life ways would have intersected often.[3] To the Norse, this lack of structures, fences, and such would have also suggested that the land was ripe for settlement, so the cultural conflict would have been repeated again and again.

SAMI SPIRITUALITY

The Sami had their own deities, both masculine and feminine. Their goddesses included an ancestral Mother Goddess Máttaráhkká, who was a female counterpart to their supreme male god, Ráddiolmmái. Máttaráhkká is closely allied with her three daughters. One daughter, Sáráhkká, "opening or cleaving" "woman/mother/wife," was a fertility goddess who formed the baby's physical body to enrobe the spirit. Her sister Uksáhkká, was the "door woman/mother/wife" who lived under entrance portals and protected them, and another sister Juoksáhkká or "bow woman/mother/wife" protected the back of the home. She also wielded a man's hunting weapon and so could be petitioned to produce male children, since in Sami belief all fetuses start life as female in Sáráhkká's image. She is therefore a goddess of transformation and change. Collectively, they are involved with nature's renewal, transformations, and protection as well as all phases of human existence. In this we can see echoes of the elder Mother Goddess from prehistory, which suggests that the Old Europeans and Sami may have shared an ancestral myth structure in the deep past.

As with other hunter-gatherer groups, the Sami spiritual landscape is populated by many supernatural denizens who enliven and enrich the physical world. Natural forces like lightning and thunder were personified as deities. The spirits of animals and birds were considered to be elder relatives, while the stones, rivers, and high mountains were beings that the people honored as *saajuv* (in the South Sami language), a term that simultaneously refers to a place and living entity. These were spirits of place. When expressed as entities, these saajuv were capable of revealing themselves in either a human or animal form and could be used by many noaide as collaborators in their work.

The Sami noaide also worked with various "Master" or "Owner" spirits of the animals. This is a concept that is common across many Siberian tribes and stretches as far eastward as the Amur River region of Russia. These master spirits can be species specific or be a general guardian of the animals—particularly of those who were hunted by people. These spirits would offer protection and oversee the human hunters to make sure they were honoring the precious gifts of his or her children.

SAMI SHAMANS

The Sami shaman, or noaide, would have served their communities by providing their own versions of divinatory and efficatory shamanic services. They were responsible for communing with the spirits and assigned the roles of keeping harmony between the worlds and caring for the physical and spiritual health of the people, of the reindeer, and of those animals that were hunted or fished for food.

In his work a male noaide would use a drum in a similar manner to Siberian peoples but also used the vocal tradition known as *joiking* to accompany shamanic trance. Female choruses or sometimes one singer

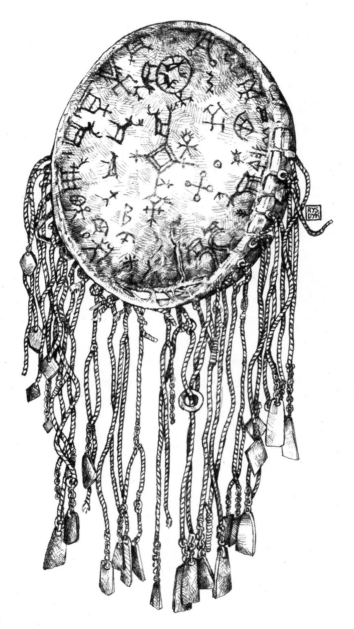

Figure 9.1. The Sami shamans used drums extensively along
with joik vocalizations to attain trance, whereas the Norse völur
used varðlokur chanting that may have been accompanied
by the rhythmic banging of iron staffs fitted with jingles
and the wielding of iron rattles.

would sing the joiks that guided the shaman into trance, kept the shaman on task while traveling through the spirit realms, and assisted in bringing the noaide back to ordinary reality.

While there isn't much evidence of female noaide in early accounts, there are a few mentioned in Old Norse literature and many more later on in post-medieval sources. The Sami language has many words for the different kinds of male noaide and also several for female practitioners that describe their magical abilities. These terms reveal that Sami women performed many different magical duties for their communities in similar ways that other shamans did for theirs.

It is also clear that Norse seiðkona and the Sami noaide have many similarities and serve similar roles in their communities. While we know that their cultures overlapped, it is impossible to determine for certain if one group of people informed the other's culture. What we can say is that, since shamanic spirituality is a remarkably ancient way of relating to the world, both peoples' ancestors most likely practiced shamanism in some form, as we can see parallels in both traditions to Siberian tribal shamanic practices stretching across Asia.

10

Preparing
to Perform Seiðr

The seiðr worker is one who is adept at entering trance. She, or in some cases he, was able to alter consciousness for the purpose of gaining information, to seek council with the spirits of nature or the ancestors, to work magic on behalf of the people, and to generally attend to the spiritual well-being of the community. For these reasons, a Viking Age seiðr practitioner may be considered that culture's shamanic equivalent.

It is important to note here that Norse practitioners of shamanic methods such as seiðr had many names. The following is a list of several of the titles used to describe a shamanic practitioner in Viking times.[1]

FEMALE NORSE SHAMANIC TITLES	MEANING
seiðkona	seiðr-woman
völva	seeress
spákona	a woman who prophesizes
galdrakona	a woman who employed the use of incantations or chants
MALE NORSE SHAMANIC TITLES	MEANING
seiðmaðr	seiðr-man
vitki	a male sorcerer
spámaðr	a man who prophesizes
galdramaðr	a man who employed the use of incantations or chants

ELEMENTS OF SEIÐR

Practitioners in modern Europe and in North America have reconstructed several variations of seiðr rituals.* Rather than share their methods, I would like to explore a shamanic framework for this work. While we do not have any accurate records of a Viking Age seiðr ceremony, these elements were recorded in the sagas.

The elements of seiðr include:

1. The seiðworker prepares herself or himself for the work to come, and a ritual space is prepared in advance of the ritual being performed.

2. The seiðworker sits in the seiðhjallr while practicing. This sets the practitioner "above the crowd" or, perhaps more pointedly, outside ordinary reality.

3. The seiðworker carries a staff, which may be adorned with precious stones. This is both a badge of office and an object used during the ritual.

4. The seiðworker may employ ritual clothing, including a cloak or hood.

5. The seiðworker has a group of people (most often women) who form a protective circle around her.

6. Singing seems to have been an essential element for the trance induction of the seiðworker, a prerequisite for the "seeing" or connecting with a wise ancestral spirit, which is the objective of seiðr. The seiðworker did not sing for herself but usually had a group of people (occasionally only one person) singing special spiritual songs called varðlokur.

7. Dreaming or entering a solitary state of deepened awareness—particularly in nature—is another common facet of seiðr.[2]

---

*Reading Jenny Blain's *Nine Worlds of Seid-Magic,* Diana Paxton's works at www.seidh.org and Annette Høst's work at www.shamanism.dk can give some insight into these methods.

8. While in an altered consciousness, the seiðworker receives information that would have been otherwise hidden from ordinary perception.

9. The seiðworker brings that information back to the gathered people.

10. Upon completion of her duties, the seiðworker returns to ordinary consciousness to rejoin the community.

Like shamans of other times and places, the Viking Age seers followed specific ritual and used specialized tools and songs to assist in their work. The information below addresses each of the elements of seiðr, and the exercises that follow will assist you in making preparations for exploring this ritual from a shamanic point of view.

THE SEIÐSTAFR OR VÖL

The seiðstafr or völ (see figure 8.2 on page 97) is a baton or staff that is a ritual tool of the seer. It not only functions as a symbol of office, it amplifies the spiritual power that is available to the seiðworker for her or his work. In this way it works like other shaman staffs.

Shaman staffs often function as representatives of the great World Tree that unites all the realms of existence. The World Tree—named Yggdrasil in the ancient Norse language—also acts as a hub for the circle of the cardinal directions. As a uniting principle, the central axis provides a counterbalance to the forces of chaos that are simultaneously pulling the cosmos apart into its constituent components. It may be said that the World Tree gives form to life.

Entering the World Tree is a common mode by which a shaman travels between the realms. As a representative of this great tree, an empowered shaman staff can also function as a portal through which a shaman may travel to and from the spirit world. In effect, when the shaman works with a staff she is situating herself at the spiritual center of the universe. Although this concept is as old as shamanism, current cosmological models agree with this idea. Instead of one unique, central point existing in the universe, each point is its own center. When a shaman intentionally creates a sacred space, she or he is consciously aware of its centrality in the cosmos. The shaman understands that all of creation can be accessed from this ritual center. While shamans as diverse as Nepalese jhankris and Andean *paqos* refer to their sacred, ritual space as a kind of central "control panel" for working with the energies of creation, it is the staff that literally represents the World Tree or central pillar of all spiritual realms. As the inspirited shaman or seiðworker holds her staff, she stands at the center of All That Is.

Just as spinning has symbolic parallels to the work of the Norns making and reworking reality, it also refers back to the practitioner of seiðr, who works to positively influence that which has been created by Urð and her kin. In that light, seiðstafr may be seen as both symbols of and tools for the seiðworker's role as a conscious participant in the weaving of reality. When the spirits of the ancestors and the nature spirits are engaged by the shaman, the infinitely mutable Ørlög, may be shaped. This is accomplished by the intentional working of aligned and focused consciousness or Wyrd, through the seiðr ritual.

The seiðworker's staff would have also been used to beat out rhythms on the floor for the singers of the varðlokur and to deepen the trance state in the same fashion as drumming or rattling is used in other shamanic cultures. A shorter seiðstafr might have also been used on a drum or shield being used for the same purpose.*

---

*In the "Lokasenna" of the *Poetic Edda,* Loki exchanges insults with Óðinn, accusing him of practicing the "womanly" art of seiðr. Loki taunts Óðinn with this phrase, "þic síða kóðo Sámseyo í, ok draptu á vétt sem völor." This translates to "you practiced seiðr on [the island of] Samsey, and you beat on a shield as völvas do." Since the "Lokasenna" is poetry, the word *shield* could also refer to a similarly shaped frame drum.

◈ *Creating Your Seiðstafr*

Creating a seiðstafr is a multistep process that includes choosing a branch, preparing the staff, and awakening its powers.

◈ Choosing a Branch or Sapling for Your Seiðstafr

You may not have access to a blacksmith who can make you an iron seiðstafr like those depicted in figure 8.2. Instead, you can make your seiðr staff from wood. Wooden examples of magical staffs have been found in excavations of völur graves and were typically either carved with runes or are of wood that was naturally twisted or crooked. Remember, all shamanic objects function as supportive tools of the practitioner. The type of material the staff is created from is less important than the purposeful intention with which it has been empowered and used.

For your seiðstafr, decide if you want a short or long staff. I prefer a wooden staff that is long enough to hold in both hands while I'm seated, with the bottom end of the staff resting on the floor. My tall staff is also long enough to be used as a walking stick. Staffs that are shorter could be rested on the knee or held in the crook of your arm while you are seated. As to a variety of wood, you may choose whatever your spiritual guidance suggests, but remember that it must be harvested with intentionality and caring.

1. Prepare yourself by wearing the right outdoor clothing and sturdy walking shoes. Bring your rattle or drum, your offering materials, a notebook, food, and water for yourself.
2. Go out onto land on which you have determined it is both safe and legal to harvest wood. If it is unfamiliar land, bring a map and compass or GPS receiver so that you won't get lost. It is also a good idea to let someone else know when and where you are going, to be extra safe.
3. When you get to the land, but prior to stepping onto it, call your shamanic ancestor to you along with your power animal.
4. Next, make an offering to him and then to the spirits of place, or

landvættir, and let them know of your intent. When making offerings, I variously use perfume, flower petals, cedar sprigs, cornmeal, honey, honey mead, or other alcohol. However, I also find that carrying a pocketful of birdseed is handy for such occasions. You may use whatever you normally use for an offering so long as it is safe for the creatures and plants that inhabit the woods and nearby waterways.

5. Ask the female forest keepers, or skogsrå, to support you in your work.

6. When you feel ready, alter consciousness with your drum or rattle. Connect with your shamanic ancestors, and ask him to take you to Freyja or the Earth Goddess/Shaman in one of her other forms. Ask Freyja to aid you in choosing a piece of tree for a seiðstafr. Since she is both the goddess of nature and of prophecy, all of the actions from choosing the wood to empowering the staff to performing seiðr are under her auspices.

   Here is a seven-line chant, or galdr, you can sing/speak to Freyja when you meet:

   > Freyja! All Mother, Great Goddess
   > Lady of beasts, Mistress of Nature,
   > Seer before all others,
   > You gave birth to prophecy.
   > You know the breadth and depth of Wyrd
   > And what the Norns conceal.
   > Guide me to the staff I require!

7. Once you have received Freyja's guidance, reverently step onto the land and begin connecting with the tree spirits. Each species of tree has a different energy. Notice what varieties of trees draw you and how you are being led. For instance, are you drawn to the willows bending over the river, the sturdy oaks spreading their canopies over the forest, or the fir tree bristling with cones?

8. When a specific tree has been chosen, ask that living being for permission to have some of its wood. Look around under the tree. A branch may be there ready for you to harvest. I have followed road crews who are trimming trees where the forest meets a roadway and have

found incredible lengths of birch, maple, oak, beech, and pine piled at the edge of the pavement and ready for gathering. I love that these branches and saplings, which would have been reduced to wood chips by the next round of work crews, were rescued for use in sacred work.

9. Only cut the flesh of a living tree when no other source is possible! Remember that shamans understand that every living being has spiritual sentience. Before you cut its flesh with knife or saw, make an offering and pray aloud your thanksgiving to the tree. As you are cutting, sing the tree your power song. This lets the spirit of the tree know who you are and the sacred heart-centered place from which your work flows. As you are singing, cut the branch or sapling thoughtfully. Take this action with great care and reverence. Only take what you absolutely need and no more. When you are through, leave another heartfelt offering of gratitude behind to thank the tree for its sacrifice.

Now that you have the wood for your shaman staff, it is time to dedicate it for seiðr. In all shamanic traditions I have studied, the shaman works with her spirits to enliven and empower her tools or objects for sacred purposes. In essence, this is the process of turning an "it" into a "who"!

The contemporary Danish seiðr practitioner and teacher Annette Høst* suggests that the seiðstafr was also referred to as *gandr,* a word that can mean not only staff but also spirit, ally, or magic, or all three at once. This is in alignment with the way shamans across the world see their ritual objects. They are not simply tools used in a shaman's practice; they are partners in the work.

◈ Healing the Spirit of the Staff

To begin transforming the piece of wood you have gathered into a seiðstafr, it is necessary to heal any trauma the stick received when it

---

*Annette is the cofounder of the Scandinavian Center for Shamanic Studies. Her articles on seiðr can be found at www.shamanism.dk/library.htm.

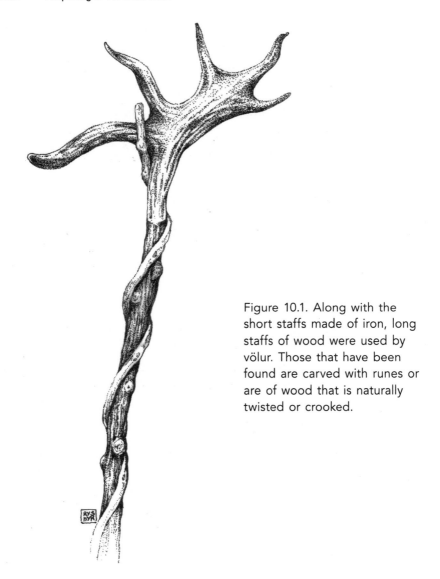

Figure 10.1. Along with the short staffs made of iron, long staffs of wood were used by völur. Those that have been found are carved with runes or are of wood that is naturally twisted or crooked.

was separated from its mother tree. To do this you will be making a journey.

You may use the fire or a rattle or drum to perform this journey-work. If neither of those options is possible, by all means feel empowered to journey with a shamanic drumming recording that includes a callback signal.

For this exercise, you will need:

- Your preferred method of providing the shamanic journey rhythm
- Your rattle
- Your blindfold
- Offering materials
- Some of your favorite food
- Your journal or a notebook and pen
- The wooden staff you gathered for your seiðstafr

1. Choose a time when you will be able to spend a long, uninterrupted time with the spirits.
2. Prepare yourself and all the materials as you did in the previous exercises. Once preparations are complete, honor the spirits of all directions and ask them to bless the area where you will be working.
3. Now call your power animal to you, and merge with the animal. This spirit will protect your spirit body on your journey.
4. Next you will make an offering to the spirits of your ancestors as a part of maintaining reverent participatory relationships with them.

    As you did before, make your offering outdoors even if you are going to be journeying inside. Begin to rattle or drum softly for a few minutes or start the recording of shamanic journey drumming. At the beginning of the journey, imagine the incredibly long line of shamanic ancestors standing behind you. Notice how they are supporting you in this journey. Thank them in advance for their assistance in working with you by making your offering. Take a small bit of your favorite food and place it on the ground. Eat a small bit of this same food yourself in communion with them.
5. Once you have made your offerings and preparations, sit in a chair with your blindfold over your eyes.
6. Hold your staff upright with the base on the floor between your feet and its top end against your forehead.
7. Call for a teacher or power animal to take you to the spirit of the tree from which your staff was harvested. (It doesn't matter if you

know what tree your staff is from or even if the tree is still living! The spirits will help you to reconnect with the spirit of the staff's original source.)

8. Enter the tree and journey down to the roots where you will see a light or feel a strong presence of the tree's life force.

9. Gather some of that light—the tree's spirit essence—to your heart.

10. As soon as you have gathered the tree's spirit essence, blow it into the top of the staff.

11. Take your rattle or drum and seal the essence into the staff. This heals any trauma the staff wood may have sustained when it was separated from its mother tree.

12. When you feel complete, be sure to thank your power animal, your shamanic ancestor, and any other spirits you met. Return fully to ordinary consciousness. Once you feel fully back from your journey, make another offering to the spirits for their loving assistance.

You may have a very clear idea of what you learned or you may have to sit with the experience for a while to understand what you were given. Allow your heart to receive the gifts and journal all that you have experienced.

◈ Discovering Your Seiðstafr's Varðlok

The wood of your staff has been healed and is now spiritually strong. At this point it can be empowered to become a seiðstafr. This is the process by which the object can become a living partner and ally in your seiðwork.

Since the staff will be used in the seiðr ceremony in which the practitioner alters her consciousness with the aid of varðlokur, now is the time to learn the song to awaken the seiðstafr. When you are acting as the völva or seiðmaðr you will use this song to dedicate it and prior to each time your seiðstafr is used in ceremony, if you are directed to do so by your spirit helpers.

As with other exercises you have done, please read all of the instructions prior to beginning to work. Gather all that is needed to ensure that you are fully prepared. Set aside time and space to do the work fully and intentionally.

For this exercise, you will need:

- Your preferred method of providing the shamanic journey rhythm
- Your rattle
- Your blindfold
- Offering materials
- Some of your favorite food
- Your journal or a notebook and pen
- The wooden staff you gathered for your seiðstafr
- An audio recorder to capture the seiðstafr song

1. Choose a time when you will be able to spend a long, uninterrupted time with the spirits. It is best if this work can be accomplished while outdoors. If that is not possible, you may work in a space that you have prepared indoors.

2. Prepare yourself and all the materials as you did in the previous exercises. Once preparations are complete, honor the spirits of all directions and ask them to bless the area where you will be working.

3. Now call your power animal to you, and merge with the animal. This spirit will protect your spirit body on your journey.

4. Next you will make an offering to the spirits of your ancestors as a part of maintaining reverent participatory relationships with them.

   As you did before, make your offering outdoors even if you are going to be journeying inside. Begin to rattle or drum softly for a few minutes or start the recording of shamanic journey drumming. At the beginning of the journey, imagine the incredibly long line of shamanic ancestors standing behind you. Notice how they are supporting you in this journey. Thank them in advance for their assistance in working with you by making your offering. Take a small bit of your favorite food and place it on the ground. Eat a small bit of this same food yourself in communion with them.

5. Once you have made your offerings and preparations, sit in a chair with your blindfold over your eyes.

6. Hold your staff upright with the base on the floor between your feet and its top end pointed toward the sky.

7. Hold a strong intention to again meet with your shamanic ancestor. Keeping this intention, honor the spirits with your song.

8. When you meet your shamanic ancestor, greet him and ask him to take you to meet Freyja the Earth Goddess and First Seiðkona.

9. Greet Freyja and thank her for agreeing to meet with you. Share that you are with her to learn the song of your seiðstafr.

10. Follow the instructions Freyja provides, and listen closely to the song she gives you. As with all spirit songs, this song may have recognizable words or use sounds instead of words.

11. Begin singing the song immediately so that you can internalize it.

12. Thank Freyja for her guidance, and return singing the song.

13. Start your audio recorder, and sing the song several times to make a recording.

14. When you feel complete, be sure to thank Freyja, your power animal, your shamanic ancestor, and any other spirits you encountered. Return fully to ordinary consciousness. Once you feel fully back from your journey, make another offering to all the spirits for their loving assistance.

You may have a very clear idea of what you learned or you may have to sit with the experience for a while to understand what you were given. Allow your heart to receive the gifts, and journal all that you have experienced.

◈ **Awakening and Binding Your Seiðstafr to You**

For this exercise, you will need:

- Your preferred method of providing the shamanic journey rhythm
- Your rattle
- Your blindfold
- Offering materials
- Some of your favorite food
- Your journal or a notebook and pen

- The wooden staff you gathered for your seiðstafr
- An audio recorder to capture the seiðstafr ritual song or varðlok

1. Again, choose a time when you will be able to spend a long, uninterrupted time with the spirits. It is best if this work can be accomplished while outdoors. If that is not possible, you may work in a space that you have prepared indoors.
2. Prepare yourself and all the materials as you did in the previous exercises. Once preparations are complete, honor the spirits of all directions, and ask them to bless the area where you will be working.
3. Now call your power animal to you, and merge with the animal. This spirit will protect your spirit body on your journey.
4. Next you will make an offering to the spirits of your ancestors as a part of maintaining reverent participatory relationships with them.

    As you did before, make your offering outdoors even if you are going to be journeying inside. Begin to rattle or drum softly for a few minutes or start the recording of shamanic journey drumming. At the beginning of the journey, imagine the incredibly long line of shamanic ancestors standing behind you. Notice how they are supporting you in this journey. Thank them in advance for their assistance in working with you by making your offering. Take a small bit of your favorite food and place it on the ground. Eat a small bit of this same food yourself in communion with them.
5. Once you have made your offerings and preparations, sit in a chair with your blindfold over your eyes.
6. Hold your staff upright with the base on the floor between your feet and its top end pointed toward the sky.
7. Hold a strong intention to again meet with your shamanic ancestor. Keeping this intention, begin to sing your own power song.
8. Once you feel fully empowered, switch to singing the seiðstafr varðlok (ritual song) to your staff.
9. Allow yourself to sway gently as you are singing the song. Imagine that you and your staff are a part of the tree that unites all reality and that you are swaying gently in the wind.

10. As you sing, notice how the staff has changed into a living being and how you and the staff are becoming connected.

11. Continue singing until you feel the process of connection is complete.

12. Once you feel complete, be sure to thank your seiðstafr, your power animal, your ancestors, and any other spirits you encountered. Return fully to ordinary consciousness. Once you feel fully back from your journey, make another offering to all the spirits for their loving assistance.

Take some time to sit with your seiðstafr, and savor the experience for a while to understand all that you were given. Allow your heart to receive the gifts, and journal all that you have experienced.

Now that you have awakened your seiðstafr for the first time, it is important to spend time with it out in nature. Make time to go out walking on the land that you hold dear. This will help you to deepen the connection you have made and bathe your seiðstafr (and you) in the energies of the nature spirits. Since all shamanic work is grounded in nature it is essential to continue deepening your own relationship to the land, water, air, and creatures with which you share your world. Think of your seiðstafr and your power animal as your companions in this work!

You may also desire to decorate your seiðstafr. If you wish to do so, perform a journey to ask the spirit of the staff how it would like you to decorate it.

◈ Other Journey Explorations

◆ Journey to a teacher or power animal to ask, "What is the best way to care for my seiðstafr?" Record the content of your journey and your perceptions about what you received.

◆ Journey to your teachers and power animals to ask each of them, "How are you connected to my seiðstafr?"

After each journey, thank your power animal, your teacher, your shamanic ancestor, and whatever other spirits you meet. Then make an offering outdoors to all the helping spirits.

VARÐLOKUR: THE SEIÐR RITUAL SONGS

Now that you have learned the song to awaken your seiðstafr and have developed a strong connection with it, you are ready to explore more of the shamanic vocal components of the seiðr ritual.

There are three more songs that are important for the seiðworker to learn. The first is a personal song for entering the shamanic state of consciousness. The second will be the journey or traveling song. The third is a song to become present and grounded back in ordinary reality. This one may be thought of as a seiðr callback signal.

◈ *Getting Your Seiðr Ritual Songs*

For this exercise, you will need:
- Your preferred method of providing the shamanic journey rhythm
- Your blindfold
- Offering materials
- Some of your favorite food
- Your journal or a notebook and pen
- Your seiðstafr
- An audio recorder to capture your seiðr songs

◈ Making the Journey
1. This journey is a long one! Choose a time when you will be able to spend a long, uninterrupted time with the spirits. It is best if this work can be accomplished while outdoors. If that is not possible, you may work in a space that you have prepared indoors.
2. Prepare yourself and all the materials as you did in the previous exercises. Once preparations are complete, honor the spirits of all directions, and ask them to bless the area where you will be working.
3. Now call your power animal to you, and merge with her or him. This spirit will protect your spirit body on your journey.

4. As you did before, make your offerings outdoors to the spirits even if you are going to be journeying inside. Thank the spirits in advance for their assistance in working with you by making your offering. Take a small bit of your favorite food and place it on the ground. Eat a small bit of this same food yourself in communion with them.

5. Once you have made your offerings and preparations, sit in a chair. Start your audio recording device and also begin sounding the shamanic journey rhythm, either live or by using a recording. Place your blindfold over your eyes.

6. Hold your staff upright with the base on the floor between your feet and its top end pointed toward the sky.

7. Hold a strong intention to journey to Freyja again to learn your personal seiðr song or varðlok for entering into the shamanic state of consciousness. While keeping this intention, begin to sing your own power song to help you fill with spiritual potency.

8. Once you feel fully empowered, switch to singing the seiðstafr varðlok to awaken your staff.

9. Allow yourself to sway gently as you are singing the song. Imagine that you and your staff are a part of the tree that unites all reality and that you are swaying gently in the wind.

10. Ask the staff to carry you to your shamanic ancestor. Since you are also merged with your power animal you may ask her or him for assistance.

11. Upon meeting your shamanic ancestor, ask her to sing your song for entering the shamanic state of consciousness. This is a varðlok that will function like drumming or rattling to help you to alter consciousness and expand awareness.

12. Begin accompanying her, and sing your song aloud until you have memorized it completely. Sing loudly enough so that your song will be captured as a recording.

13. Next ask your shamanic ancestor for the journeying/traveling varðlok. This may be similar to the one that you use for attaining the shamanic state of consciousness or very different in nature.

14. Once your ancestor begins to sing, memorize the song and begin

singing it with her. Sing it repeatedly until you have internalized it, and as before, sing loudly enough to ensure the recording will be clear.

15. Now ask your fylgja for her or his varðlok. This will be the song you sing to invoke the spirit's power in any situation.

16. Finally, ask your shamanic ancestor to sing the varðlok of return, the song that will bring you back to a present and alert state of awareness in ordinary reality. Repeat it until you have it memorized, and again make sure to sing it loudly enough so that your recording will be clear.

17. Once you feel complete, be sure to thank your seiðstafr, your power animal, your ancestors, and any other spirits you encountered.

18. Continue singing the song of return, and allow it to bring you back from your journey. If you are using a recording of journey drumming, turn it off and continue singing your returning song until you feel grounded and present.

19. Once you feel fully back from your journey, make another offering to all the spirits for their loving assistance.

Take some time to sit with your seiðstafr and savor the experience for a while to understand all that you were given. Allow your heart to receive the gifts, and journal all that you have experienced.

Practice with your recording until you can easily remember all of the songs you have learned. This is essential, as they will allow you to perform song-supported journeys and the seiðr ritual safely. To be able to enter into the shamanic state of consciousness and to return at will are the hallmarks of any shaman. To do so with the song and staff is the hallmark of the seiðkona or seiðmaðr. In addition, if you will eventually use a support chorus like the Viking Age seeresses, you will have to know these songs well enough to teach them to those singers.

THE SEIÐR HOOD AND CLOAK

All the shamans with whom I have studied have special ritual clothing that they don whenever they are going to perform healings or other ritual work. Since a shaman's ritual clothing is empowered or enlivened, it holds power. When the shaman puts on the clothing she begins to shift into an altered state of awareness. By putting these pieces of attire on the body, she is in effect beginning to merge with the spirit power held within it. For many, the clothing is awakened in a similar manner as you do when you work with your staff. A shaman sings to all of her shamanic paraphernalia before beginning to work and feels the objects awakening during the song. In essence, this is part of gathering all of the shaman's spirit helpers for the task at hand.

At its foundation, the seiðr hood and cloak function like the shaman's costume. They are not only badges of office, they are empowered allies or gandr that accompany and assist the shaman during the seiðr ritual. The hood and cloak are common garments during the medieval period that were worn across Eurasia. While other Viking garments are unique, the hood and cloak were so functional that in spite of small regional differences, they are nearly universal. The cloak functions like a coat, whereas the hood functions not only to cover the head but also to provide an extra layer of protection to the shoulders. This would have been especially important in the damp and cold weather of Scandinavia. It is also very useful to keep one more comfortable during útiseta.

For the seiðr ritual, the hood can be pulled down over the eyes. This has the dual purpose of screening out ordinary reality distractions and also to hide the face of the seiðworker from others while she prophesizes. When the face of the seiðkona is hidden, the voice sounds somewhat disembodied, and the effect on those gathered can be much more powerful.

You may choose to purchase your cloak and hood* from reputable

---

*An excellent resource for incredible and beautifully made historical (medieval through Renaissance) garments may be found through the company Moresca, in upstate New York. They have a quirky website, but the degree of craftsmanship of their period clothing is extraordinary and worth the nuisance of using their site at www.moresca.com/index.php. (If, due to cost or available time, you can only procure or create one of these ritual garments at a time, begin with a seiðr hood.)

craftspeople who create medieval period garments or who specifically specialize in Viking Age clothing. Another option is to make these articles of clothing yourself. A traditional material for these articles is wool fabric. I have two hoods; one is of a heavy wool of the type that would be used for a coat, while the other is of a loose wool weave that is still opaque enough to screen out the light but more bearable for wearing indoors.

Simple instructions for creating your own hood can be found in appendix B of this book.

◈ *Empowering Your Seiðr Hood and Cloak*

For this exercise, you will need:

- Your preferred method of providing the shamanic journey rhythm
- Offering materials
- Some of your favorite food
- Your journal or a notebook and pen
- Your seiðstafr
- Your new seiðr hood and cloak
- An audio recorder to capture new varðlokur offered by spirit

◈ Making the Journey

1. As you have done before, choose a time when you will be able to spend a long, uninterrupted time with the spirits. It is best if this work can be accomplished while outdoors. If that is not possible, you may work in a space that you have prepared indoors.

2. Make your offerings outdoors to the spirits even if you are going to be journeying inside. Thank the spirits in advance for their assistance in working with you by making your offering. Take a small bit of your favorite food and place it on the ground. Eat a small bit of this same food yourself in communion with them.

3. Prepare yourself and all the materials as you did in the previous exercises. Once preparations are complete, honor the spirits of all

directions, and ask them to bless the area where you will be working.

4. Now call your power animal to you and sing its varðlok. Allow the song to deepen your connection. When you feel ready, merge with the animal. This spirit will protect your spirit body on your journey.

5. Once you have made your offerings and preparations, don your garments and sit in a chair and hold your seiðstafr.

6. Start your audio recording device and also begin playing the shamanic journey rhythm or singing your varðlok for entering into the shamanic state of consciousness. Place your hood down over your eyes.

7. Once you have entered the shamanic state of consciousness, begin singing your journeying/traveling varðlok.

8. Travel again to Freyja in her guise as the First Shaman.

9. Ask Freyja to merge with you for the purposes of empowering your garments. Since you are also merged with your power animal, the energy of Freyja will be tempered for your physical body.

10. Allow Freyja's spiritual energy to infuse your garments.

11. When Freyja has completed her work, thank her, unmerge, and begin to sing your varðlok of return. This is the song that will bring you back to a present and alert state of awareness in ordinary reality. Repeat it until you feel grounded back in ordinary reality.

12. Remove your hood from your eyes.

Once you feel fully back from your journey, make another offering to all the spirits for their loving assistance.

Take some time to sit with your seiðr hood and cloak to savor the experience for a while and to understand all that you were given. Allow your heart to receive the gifts, and journal all that you have experienced.

◈ Other Journey Explorations

- ◆ Journey to a teacher or power animal to ask, "What are the ways I am to use this hood and cloak in my shamanic practice?" Record the content of your journey and your perceptions about what you received.

- Journey to a teacher or power animal to ask her or him: "What is the best way to care for my seiðr garments?"

After each journey, thank your power animal, your teacher, your shamanic ancestor, and whatever other spirits you meet. Then make an offering outdoors to all the helping spirits.

◈ **Process Questions**
- Write down in your journal what it was like to empower your garments.
- How does it feel to have these new tools support your process? Record your impressions.
- As with all of your other shamanic ritual items, journey to find out how these garments need to be cared for and stored.

PREPARING THE SPACE FOR A COMMUNITY SEIÐR CEREMONY

There are a few essential elements that are necessary for performing a safe and powerful shamanic ceremony.

Having Clear Intentions

This is the beginning place for all rituals. Selecting a focus and setting your intention for your ceremony will determine the way it unfolds. For a ceremony that includes others, it is especially necessary to have a razor-clear intent. This allows all the participants to more fully contribute their energy and excitement to the desired outcome. This is especially important in a seiðr ritual in that the participants will be contributing to holding space, assisting you to enter trance, recording information you access from spirit, and assisting in your return to ordinary reality.

Clearing and Preparing the Space

When setting the stage for a formal ritual, the work space needs to be cleared and dedicated to its purpose. This work should be done with a light heart that is honoring the sacredness of the task. Make sure that the space only contains what contributes to the ceremony.

As well as a physical cleaning, it is important to include a way to clear out any heavy or sluggish spiritual energy present in the space. Wafting smoke around the space from burning special plants such as sage or incense is one method; however, it is the intent and the feelings you hold while engaging in the activity that generate the shifts in energy.

At this point the seiðkona's high seat can be set up. This can be as simple as an armchair set in a prominent area, or if space allows, it can be an elaborate chair and platform constructed and dedicated exclusively for this purpose. Remember to clear the chair and platform as you did with the room.

Once it is cleared, it is important to program the space for the task to come. As I finish with a clearing, I envision—again in my feeling body—the action that is to happen. For instance, if the space is to be used for a wedding, I feel the couple lovingly embracing, happily moving through their lives together, and surrounded by those who love them. In feeling the ritual as if it were already underway, I am not only programming the space but also alerting the helpful and healing spirits to what is about to unfold. That naturally leads me to the next element of ritual, which is the calling together of the spirits who will be participating in the ceremony.

Honoring the Seen and Unseen—Calling Together the Participants

It is important to be clear about whom you wish to participate in your ceremony. If the participants are physical human beings, then you send an invitation that includes a clear intent for the ritual. When they arrive, you honor them with gratitude for their presence and participation. Unseen guests require the same kind of attention. For a seiðr ritual this may be done with a spirit-calling varðlok. As a shaman or seiðworker your intentions must be very clear that the spirits you are calling are only helpful, healing spirits. Always invoke your known guardians and power animals first so that they can assist in keeping the space clear of any intrusive energy.

Opening the Ceremony

Once the setting is ready and all the participants are welcomed, it is important to officially open the ceremony. This element of the ceremony communicates clearly to all who are choosing to be with you that you are about to begin. Sometimes this can be as simple as asking all present to share a moment of breath. They may be asked to imagine that they are all breathing one single breath with many bodies; every being who has gathered for the ceremony becomes unified into a coalesced whole. After this, the ceremony begins in earnest.

This is a wonderful opportunity to offer a prayer, a declaration of intent, or traditional Viking-style galdr. Galdr are clear, often poetically phrased intentions or incantations that are spoken aloud. They are usually spoken forcefully and with passion. Intentions manifested in this way can have great power. Here is an example I've written that you may wish to use as a way to declare the ritual has begun:

> *Here at the center of all the worlds,*
> *Here at the Great Tree, Yggdrasil,*
> *We give thanks for fertile Ørlög*
> *And the workings of Wyrd,*
> *Which manifests all things.*
> *We honor the Wise Ones!*
> *And their powers teach and heal!*

After this, the chorus would begin singing the varðlok that assists the seiðworker to attain the shamanic state of consciousness.

Directing the Flow

As the ceremony proceeds, it is important to inform the participants of each step. The seiðworker may be able to do this since nearly all of the ritual is done while speaking aloud. However, having a designated assistant is very beneficial to assist in keeping the participants on task while the seiðworker is in trance.

Making Closure

Just as a clear beginning is an important aspect of ceremony, so is a clear point of closure. Once the seiðworker has sung her return varðlok and has returned to ordinary consciousness, it is important to thank the nonphysical beings and let them know that your work together is done. Let yourself be filled with gratitude as you thank them for their participation, releasing them back into their normal flow. At this point, the physical humans who have gathered for the ceremony begin their return back to their ordinary consciousness, too. Honor the human participants for their willingness to participate and share a snack or meal together. If the content of the ceremony is to be processed or interpreted, this is a good time to do so. This helps them to ground back into their bodies so they are more able to safely engage in tasks like traveling home!

◆ Receiving Varðlokur for a Community Seiðr Ceremony

Each aspect of the seiðr ritual is guided by a different varðlok. The following exercises will guide you through journeys in which you will receive these songs. By recording them and then repeating them several times, you will be able to internalize them as you go along. As you have done with other exercises, read them all the way through before you begin.

◆ Receiving a Varðlok for Calling the Helpful Spirits

For this exercise, you will need:
- Your preferred method of providing the shamanic journey rhythm
- Your seiðr hood and cloak

- Offering materials
- Some of your favorite food
- Your journal or a notebook and pen
- Your seiðstafr
- An audio recorder to capture the new varðlok offered by spirit

1. As before, choose a time when you will be able to spend a long, uninterrupted time with the spirits. It is best if this work can be accomplished while outdoors. If that is not possible, you may work in a space that you have prepared indoors.
2. Make your offerings outdoors to the spirits even if you are going to be journeying inside. Thank the spirits in advance for their assistance in working with you by making your offering. Take a small bit of your favorite food and place it on the ground. Eat a small bit of this same food yourself in communion with them.
3. Prepare yourself and all the materials as you did in the previous exercises. Once preparations are complete, honor the spirits of all directions, and ask them to bless the area where you will be working.
4. Now call your power animal to you, and merge with the animal. This spirit will protect your spirit body on your journey.
5. Once you have made your offerings and preparations, don your garments and sit in a chair with your seiðstafr.
6. Start your audio recording device, and also begin singing your varðlok for entering into the shamanic state of consciousness. Place your hood down over your eyes.
7. Once you have entered the shamanic state of consciousness, begin singing your journeying/traveling varðlok.
8. Travel again to Freyja in her guise as the First Shaman.
9. Ask Freyja to teach you the varðlok for calling the helpful spirits for the seiðr ritual.
10. Once you have learned it, begin to sing it aloud so that you can remember and record the song.
11. When Freyja has completed her work, thank her for the spirit-calling

varðlok, and begin to sing your varðlok of return—the song that will bring you back to a present and alert state of awareness. Thank your power animal. Repeat your return varðlok until you feel grounded back in ordinary reality.

12. Remove your hood from your eyes.

Once you feel fully back from your journey, make another offering to all the spirits for their loving assistance.

Take some time to savor the experience for a while and to understand all that you were given. Allow your heart to receive the gifts and journal all that you have experienced.

◈ Receiving a Varðlok or Galdr for Thanking and Releasing the Helpful Spirits

To be able to complete the seiðr ritual, you will also need to have a varðlok (song) or galdr (poetic chant) for thanking and releasing the spirits that gathered for your ritual. The releasing of spirits is done with the same reverence and care that you offered in calling them together.

For this exercise, you will need:

- ♦ Your preferred method of providing the shamanic journey rhythm
- ♦ Your hood and cloak
- ♦ Offering materials
- ♦ Some of your favorite food
- ♦ Your journal or a notebook and pen
- ♦ Your seiðstafr
- ♦ An audio recorder to capture the new varðlok or galdr offered by spirit

1. As you've done before, make preparations and place offerings outdoors to the spirits even if you are going to be journeying inside.
2. Prepare yourself and all the materials as you did in the previous exercises. Once preparations are complete, honor the spirits, thanking them for blessing the area where you will be working.

3. Now call your power animal to you, and sing its varðlok. Allow the song to deepen your connection. When you feel ready, merge with the animal. This spirit will protect your spirit body on your journey.

4. Once you have made your offerings and preparations, don your garments and sit in a chair with your seiðstafr.

5. Start your audio recording device, and also begin singing your varðlok for entering into the shamanic state of consciousness. Place your hood down over your eyes.

6. Once you have entered the shamanic state of consciousness, begin singing your journeying/traveling varðlok.

7. Travel again to Freyja in her guise as the First Shaman.

8. Ask Freyja to teach you the varðlok or galdr for releasing the helpful spirits at the end of the seiðr ritual.

9. Once you have learned it, begin to sing it aloud so that you can remember and record the song.

10. When Freyja has completed her work, thank her for the spirit-releasing varðlok or the galdr that she provided. Begin to sing your varðlok of return. Continue to sing your return varðlok until you feel grounded back in ordinary reality. Once you are fully back to the present moment and have achieved an alert state of awareness, thank your power animal.

11. Remove your hood from your eyes.

Make another offering to all the spirits for their loving assistance, and take time to record your experience in your journal.

As you have done with all the previous steps, take some time to savor the experience for a while and to understand all that you were given. Allow your heart to savor the gifts you have received.

◈ Other Journey Explorations

- ◆ Journey to a teacher or power animal to ask, "What are the ways I am to use this spirit-releasing varðlok/galdr in my shamanic practice?" Record the content of your journey and your perceptions about what you received.

After each journey, thank your power animal, your teacher, your shamanic ancestor, and whatever other spirits you meet. Then make an offering outdoors to all the helping spirits.

◈ **Process Questions**
  ◆ Write down in your journal what it was like to honor/ release the spirits with song.
  ◆ Record your impressions about how you feel when you sing each of the varðlokur you have learned. Notice sensations, emotional feelings, and any other ways you are aware that you change with each song or chant.

11

Other Accoutrements of the Völva

While the high seat, staff, and hood are the most common trappings associated with Old Norse seers, these shamans may have employed other magical objects while performing their work.

MASKS

While the use of a hood to shield the eyes for trance would have been an essential feature of the seiðkona's ritual garb, there is some archaeological evidence that suggests that some practitioners may have also used animal masks.[1] There are several different reasons a völva may have chosen to wear a mask. A mask can be useful in deepening a trance state; it alters the wearer's appearance so that the transformation into a shamanic spiritual ally, in this case an animal, is deepened, and it assists the shaman's helping spirits to more strongly enter this physical realm. More plainly put, wearing a mask while performing seiðr activities could have supported a more powerful experience.

From Hedeby in northern Germany, which was once a great Danish Viking city, to Novgorod, which lies 120 miles south of St. Petersburg in Russia, numerous animal masks have been unearthed across the former Viking territory. Created from thick wool felt and leather, these flexible masks would have covered all or most of the wearer's face.

There are curious figures on the tapestry found buried with the Oseberg völur. These include images of women with animal heads.[2] One figure is shown with a boar's head and the boar's raised ridge of bristles running down the figure's back. The other figure has the head of a bird and is posed in a position that suggests that she has folded wings.

These masks and those woven images from the Oseberg tapestry may provide evidence of the use of masks being used during ritual practice. In addition, the profound practice of merging with and taking on the attributes of one's power animal or fylgja would be very beneficial to those völur who were engaged in potentially dangerous spiritual work. For instance, I can certainly imagine that having a deeper connection to one's protective spirits would have been very comforting while sitting on a burial mound during a wilderness questing ritual. The same would have been true while doing battle with disease-causing spirits or other spirits that harass the living. In this way, the völva would have paralleled those berserkr and *úlfheðnar* warriors who wore animal pelts (bear and wolf, respectively) and fought in a wild trance. Masks may have also contributed to the mystery and power of the seiðr ritual, as the seiðkona would have been even more otherworldly while both masked and hooded.

SHAPE-SHIFTING

The act of becoming another being is a part of shamanic practice. Merging with a spirit is how we share power to accomplish the work we have been called to do. All spiritual merging with teachers or power animals is a part of shape-shifting or shape changing. It is also true that the merging can be more or less intense based on the situation. For instance, I merge with my fylgja every morning for protection from unbeneficial energies. This shape-shifting is light enough for me to function well in ordinary life. When I am doing healing, I deepen my connection and have more powerful experiences of my power animal, feeling sensations of our muzzle, of our claws, and that my physical body has doubled

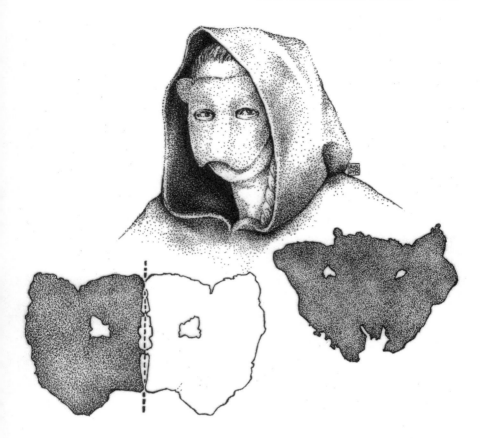

Figure 11.1. The purpose of wool felt masks excavated from
the Viking port of Hedeby is unknown; however, they may have
been used in shamanic rituals or to enhance shape-shifting,
or *hamingja*, by a völva. The mask on the left in this drawing
was found incomplete and so is shown with its right half as a mirror
image of the portion of the artifact that was found.

in size. A deeper, total immersion in the spirit of one's fylgja might be
necessary for working with especially powerful or frightening spirits,
such as the wandering spirits of violent deceased people, the entity of a
dangerous disease, or in other situations where the life of the völva may
be in jeopardy.

Traditionally, fylgjur could be wild animals such as a fox, wolves,
polar bears, deer, brown bears, serpents, eagles, falcons, hawks, swans

or other birds, reindeer, ocean mammals, and even lions and leopards that the Vikings met on their extensive travels. Particularly strong or tenacious domestic animals such as a boar, oxen, or a billy goat* could also be a fylgja, as could those creatures we think of as mythical, such as dragons and other fantastic creatures.

Norse stories are filled with examples of people who change shape to accomplish tasks and solve serious problems. By taking on the attributes of a fierce creature, one could tap into the strength, cunning, or other talent of the animal to augment the individual's ordinary power. Old Norse skaldic poetry is filled with many animal-related, metaphoric compound phrases called *kennings*. These are peculiarly poetic ways to describe the attributes or nature of people, their body parts, weapons, and other objects. These are like the honorific euphemisms that circumpolar people in shamanic cultures use to describe particularly sacred animals. For instance, metaphoric names such as "Forest Apple," "Honey Paw," "Old Man of the Mountain," and "Winter Sleeper" were used to speak about the bear. This animal was thought of as a messenger to the spiritual realms and mediator with the "Lord of the Forest" who, when ceremonially killed and honored, could ensure that there would be enough game animals to feed the people. Due to the bear's high status, it was never referred to by its common name.

During the Viking Age, this roundabout way of speaking was used to describe power objects such as effective swords, "Wolf of Wounds," or axes such as "Bone-Beak." The sword arm of a powerful warrior might be "Feeder of Ravens," alluding to the ravens that feed on battleground corpses. A ship might be called a "Sea-Steed," while the sea itself would be referred to as the "Whale Road." Jötunn were referred to as "Mountain Wolves" and Oðinn is known as "Battle-Wolf," "Eagle-Head," and "Raven God." More than simple descriptions, these honorific kennings conveyed a sense that the objects or beings they indicated exhibited traits that were usually ascribed to animals. This certainly has

---

*The god Thor (Þór) rode across the sky in a chariot drawn by two goats, Tanngrisnir and Tanngnjóstr.

Figure 11.2. This wooden polar bear mask represents the fylgja or power animal of the shaman who wears it. Shamanic artist Hib Sabin carved this mask of juniper wood, then decorated it with paint, wax, and leather straps. (Private collection.)

resonance with the older shamanic use of euphemisms and may be seen as a way to suggest their otherworldly aspects.

TALISMANS OR TAUFR

Every shaman grave that has been unearthed has contained charms and talismans that were a part of that practitioner's ritual goods. Talismanic objects can be a part of her personal attire, featured on her altars, or deemed essential to her working environment. These objects could be used to bring game animals to the hunters, to honor personal or clan ancestors, to strengthen the connection to a deity or spiritual teacher, or be part of a shaman's personal protection.

Figure 11.3. Animal teeth, claws, owl pellets, shells,
crystals, and other objects have been associated
with shaman burials.

A collection of taufr might include a crystal, an animal bone, an ancestral object, a feather, special beads, shells, stones, and any other objects with potent meaning for the völva. Any of these objects might embody the spirit of the shaman's helping spirits, connect them to the land from which they draw power, provide protection, provide a portal for spirits to enter this world, and be used in divination or healing. Some talismans can be worn as visible decoration as one might wear jewelry, while others would be kept hidden until they are needed for the seiðkona's magical work.

If you are drawn to include objects as a part of your sacred paraphernalia, be certain that spirit is calling you to gather, empower, and use them. In Western culture, we have grown to believe that objects make the shaman. Instead, talismans, ritual attire, staffs, and drums should be reflective of the working relationships we create and nurture with the spirits. They also do not need to be elaborate or beautiful to hold power for us. Indeed, a small stone or shell can hold as much shamanic power as the most elaborate, jewel-like creation. It is the spiritual energy in the object that matters most for the one who wields it.

Figure 11.4. This small silver charm is thought to
represent Freyja and the circle of her necklace, Brisingamen,
which was created from energies gathered from
the four corners of the world.

◈ *Journey to Shape-Shift into Your Power Animal, or Fylgja*

For this exercise, you will need:

- ◆ Your preferred method of providing the shamanic journey rhythm
- ◆ Offering materials
- ◆ Some of your favorite food
- ◆ Your journal or a notebook and pen

- ◆ Your seiðstafr
- ◆ Your new seiðr hood and cloak

◈ Making the Journey

1. Give yourself a long, uninterrupted time with the spirits. It is best if this work can be accomplished while outdoors. If that is not possible, you may work in a space that you have prepared indoors.
2. As you did before, make your offerings outdoors to the spirits even if you are going to be journeying inside. Thank the spirits in advance for their assistance in working with you by making your offering. Take a small bit of your favorite food and place it on the ground. Eat a small bit of this same food yourself in communion with them.
3. Prepare yourself and all the materials as you did in the previous exercises. Once preparations are complete, honor the spirits of all directions, and ask them to bless the area where you will be working.
4. Start your audio recording device, and also begin playing the shamanic journey rhythm or singing your varðlok for entering into the shamanic state of consciousness. Place your hood down over your eyes.
5. Now call your power animal to you and sing its varðlok. Allow the song to deepen your connection. When you feel ready, merge with the animal. This spirit will protect your spirit body on your journey.
6. Once you have entered the shamanic state of consciousness, begin singing your journeying/traveling varðlok.
7. Travel to the place that is your fylgja's home.
8. Once there, ask the power animal to show you how to deepen your merging to shape-shift.
9. Allow yourself to fully experience these sensations.
10. When the experience is complete, thank your fylgja for the lesson and ask, "How should I use this deepened experience of your power?"
11. Once you feel complete, unmerge and begin to sing your varðlok of return. This is the song that will bring you back to a present and alert state of awareness in ordinary reality. Repeat it until you feel grounded back in ordinary reality.

12. Remove your hood from your eyes.

13. Once you feel fully back from your journey, make another offering to all the spirits for their loving assistance.

Take some time to sit to savor the experience for a while and to understand all that you were given. Allow your heart to receive the gifts and journal all that you have experienced.

◈ Seiðr Mask Journey Explorations

If you feel called to include a mask in your seiðr paraphernalia or to deepen your experience of shape-shifting, it is best to journey to your helping spirits to ask what you might wear, how the spirit would like to be depicted, and how the mask is to be used.

- Journey to a teacher or power animal to ask, "What is the importance for me of wearing a mask while I perform seiðr?"
- If you find out that a mask would be useful to you, do another journey to ask, "What spirit will my seiðr mask represent?"
- You may also wish to ask, "What is the way for me to create a seiðr mask?" Finally, once your mask is completed, follow the instructions outlined in the previous chapters to empower your mask for use.

Record the content of your journeys and your perceptions about what you received. Remember that, as with all other shamanic tools, once your mask is empowered, it is alive and must be cared for with intentionality. After each journey, thank your power animal, your teacher, your shamanic ancestor, and whatever other spirits you meet. Then make an offering outdoors to all the helping spirits.

◈ Other Journey Explorations

- Journey to a teacher or fylgja to ask, "What objects are important for me to include in my seiðr practice?"

- If you find out that an object or talisman would be useful to you, do other journeys to ask, "What does this object represent for me?" and "What is the best way to empower it for use?"
- You may also wish to ask, "What is the best way for me to care for this object?"

Record the content of your journeys and your perceptions about what you received. After each journey, thank your teacher and whatever other spirits you meet. Then make an offering outdoors to all the helping spirits.

12

Útiseta

Connecting with Nature's Power

Wilderness vision questing is an ancient, cross-cultural practice that involves spending time alone in nature while fasting. It is a spiritual tradition that has been practiced for millennia by people seeking to receive revelation and to reconnect to nature, to the spirits—especially ancestral spirits—and with their deeper selves.[1] This time of deep introspection in nature has many beneficial effects on the psyche and the spirit.

During the Viking Age, the útiseta, or "sitting out," ritual was specifically used to commune with the spirits of the natural world and the spirits of the dead for divinatory purposes. However, this ritual is especially vital for the twenty-first-century practitioner as we experience a deep cultural separation from nature. This disconnection weakens our individual connection to power. Without making intentional, undistracted forays into the natural world, we become like rechargeable devices that have spent too long without being plugged into an electrical outlet. We become weak and ineffective, not only in our spiritual practice but also in our ordinary lives.

Spending time alone in nature allows us to be replenished. We refresh our passion for living and consciously reconnect ourselves to the larger web of life. Since most of our species' time on the Earth was spent outside, we also reconnect ourselves to the thousands of generations that

Figure 12.1. The simple beauty of a blue jay feather picked up on a walk or during an útiseta can become a talisman for fostering connection with nature and the helper spirits.

have gone before us. When we immerse ourselves back into the natural world, we experience awe. As we become reacquainted with the beauty of the world, we simultaneously feel a profound connectedness with All That Is and develop humility about our tiny place within it. This in turn nurtures a sense of reverence for the natural world and sparks a desire to protect Mother Earth from our collective desire to exploit her resources.

Wilderness questing provides several layers of benefits.[2] They include connections to Self, personal empowerment, and connection to others. These "others" will include other humans, but more importantly, the quester experiences a much deeper connection to the natural world and its spirits. Increasing degrees of connection to the Self can include self-discovery and a deeper sense of purpose. In addition, a stronger sense of clarity, awareness, and self-acceptance may begin to unfold.

The stronger connection with Self generates a sense of empowerment. In facing any fears that may arise during the time in nature, a trust grows in the Self, in nature, and in the quester's spiritual resources. Confidence at having performed the ritual generates powerful feelings of inner strength.

As a person gains confidence with the Self, with the spirits, and with nature, a profound feeling of connectedness often blossoms. The quester feels a palpable sense of connection to nature and the other beings who share the planet. Deep healings can occur and a desire to work in community for the greater good may also be stimulated.

These benefits occur even in those people who do not practice any form of shamanism. This is because we are all a part of nature. It is only an illusion that we are in any way separate from other beings or nature as a whole. When we reintroduce ourselves to our original context, we begin to feel more enlivened, awake, and aware than ever before. For the person with a strong spiritual practice, the effects can be even more powerful.

As I wrote in a previous chapter, a seiðworker's vision questing would entail sitting outside overnight while holding the seiðstafr and wearing the cloak and hood. To be safe, the quester would also be merged with their protective spirits to remain protected from any unbeneficial wandering souls. The quester's protectors might be a power animal (fylgja), a female protector spirit (dis), or a familiar ancestral spirit. The seiðworker would sing and chant in concert with the elements, animals, birds, and transcendent nature spirits or landvættir. If the útiseta was being performed in the forest, the skogsrå (female forest keeper) would also be contacted, and the practitioner would provide an offering to the land wights' willingness to participate. Our ancestors understood that these beings were guardians of the land and were also capable of sharing a great deal of wisdom, so caring for them would have been seen as a way to ensure a good life.

During the útiseta, the seiðworker would use her varðlok for awakening the staff, for gathering the helpful spirits, and for entering into the shamanic state of consciousness. During the course of the útiseta, the quester would continue to sing her experiences and offer galdr (incantations or poetic songs) to the spirits. These periods of singing and chanting would be alternated with long periods of silence to receive the spirits' wisdom and to feel the connections being woven with the unseen and the natural worlds.

At this point in your training, it is important to perform the úti-seta. To prepare for this time of sitting out in nature, it is important to clarify your purpose. This ritual can be used to spiritually prepare for a transition, ritual; or event; to regain clarity when life has become confusing; to connect with an ancestor to gain her or his insight; to inspirit yourself after a long illness or traumatic situation; to reconnect to your home spirits after traveling; or to strengthen your ties with your power animals, teachers, and nature. While vision-questing ceremonies like útiseta can last over the course of several days, with proper preparation and a strong intention it is possible to have a powerful experience over the course of one night.

PREPARING FOR ÚTISETA

To prepare for the ritual, you will need to find a place in nature where you will be safe. It is also best to let someone you trust know where you will be. The wilder the space you have your útiseta the better, but work within the parameters that your life and physical abilities require. The idea is to find a place where you can safely experience nature's vital-ity. You will likely experience some discomfort during your sitting out time, but it is not necessary to suffer! For instance, while most folks can easily sit on a folded wool blanket or ground cloth during an útiseta, I have mobility limitations that interfere with me getting down on the ground. For this reason, I have a folding camp chair that I ritually set up for an útiseta. I alternate being seated and standing over the course of the night. My body is still uncomfortable, but I am not suffering. Another concern in my area is the many deer ticks infected with Lyme disease. For this reason, I use an insect repellent as a part of my prepa-ration. Since you may need to relieve yourself during the night, bring what you need for that purpose, as well.

The idea is to find a kind of balance. You need to be uncomfort-able enough that you won't drop off to sleep but not so uncomfortable or anxious that you can't remain in ceremony all night. An útiseta

Figure 12.2. The act of taking oneself outside away from people and immersed in nature is a powerful way to refresh and deepen the connection with spirit helpers, as well as with the spirits of the beloved ancestors. Like the wilderness quests of other shamanic cultures, an útiseta can help to clarify a seiðworker's purpose and provide visions that are necessary for their continued empowerment.

begins just before sunset and ends with the sun's rise over the horizon. In the morning, eat lightly and drink plenty of water to rehydrate yourself. You also want to have time to record and assimilate your experience afterward. Make sure you can have a few hours of uninterrupted time to allow the experience to be fully anchored in your being.

Once you have chosen your spot to perform útiseta, do the following journey as preparation.

◈ *Útiseta Journeys*

The following exercises will continue your preparations for a safe and effective útiseta experience. The first exercise below is a journey accompanied by your power animal to introduce yourself to the spirits of the place where you will be sitting out. Then you will be ready to perform your útiseta! For your útiseta, choose a time and space that will support you to have the best experience possible. In the exercise on page 159 the útiseta will be to meet with Freyja to ask her to share your personal varðlok. This is the song by which the spirits recognize you. It is the song of your soul. Since you will *not* be recording your song as you have done before, you must sing it until you completely internalize it. Singing your song can be incredibly powerful, and you may feel shifts and changes inside as you do so.

◈ Útiseta Preparation Journey

1. Journey to your teacher or power animal to ask her or him to take you to meet with the spirits of place where you will be performing your útiseta.
2. Once you meet them introduce yourself and ask, "What is your name?"
3. Once you have gotten acquainted ask, "How may I honor you so that I may perform útiseta in your home in safety?"
4. Record the content of your journey and your perceptions about what you received.

◈ Performing Útiseta to Learn Your Personal Varðlok

For this exercise, you will need:

- Prepared ritual space including a folded wool blanket to act as your cushion, or if you need to be off the ground, you may use a camp chair
- A flashlight
- Your seiðr hood and cloak
- Your seiðstafr
- Offering materials
- Food and drink to be ingested the morning after the ritual
- Your journal or a notebook and pen

1. Choose a time and space that will allow you to spend a safe and uninterrupted night with the spirits. Prepare all that you need for your ritual ahead of time so that it can go smoothly.
2. On the day of your útiseta, prepare your ritual space. Make your offerings, and thank the spirits in advance for their assistance. Take a small bit of your favorite food and place it on the ground to feed your spirit companions.
3. Put on your cloak and hood.
4. Take your place on your blanket or chair, and hold your seiðstafr.
5. Sing the varðlok for awakening your seiðstafr.
6. Sing the varðlok for calling the helpful spirits for the útiseta.
7. Now call your power animal to you, and merge with the animal. This spirit will protect your spirit body as you journey.
8. Begin singing your varðlok for entering into the shamanic state of consciousness.
9. Once you are in the shamanic state of consciousness, begin singing your journeying/traveling varðlok.
10. Travel again to Freyja, the First Shaman.
11. Once you meet Freyja, ask her to share your personal varðlok with you.
12. Sing your varðlok until your memory of it and the feelings it provokes inside of you are a permanent part of your being.

13. Thank Freyja, and continue your spiritual explorations by interacting with the spirits of place, your ancestors, and any other beneficial spirits that may reveal themselves.

14. During the night also take time to allow wisdom to flow to you while you are in silence. Notice the animals and birds that are awake and active during the night. Listen to the rustling leaves, the lapping of water, and any other sounds that are around you. These are part of the varðlok of the place.

15. When the sun rises over the horizon, thank Freyja, your power animal, and any other spirits with whom you interacted. Begin to sing your varðlok of return so that you return fully to a present and alert state of awareness. Repeat your return varðlok until you feel grounded back in ordinary reality.

16. Remove your hood.

17. Once you feel fully back from your journey, make another offering to all the spirits for their loving assistance.

18. Close the ritual with a galdr for closure such as:

> I honor the Ørlög,
> Pregnant with all possibilities.
> I honor the Great Tree, Yggdrasil,
> And Urð, the embodiment of Wyrd.
> I honor Freyja the mother shaman,
> My ancestors and helping spirits;
> I thank you and release you!

Or this galdr:

> Hail Landvaettir and Husvaettir!
> Hail my Ancestors!
> Hail the Vanir! The Aesir! Our Spirit Teachers!
> I honor you all!
> Provide me your blessings and protection.
> Hail helpful, healing spirits of the Nine Realms!
> Go peacefully back to your homes with my gratitude.

Take some time to savor the experience for a while and to understand all that you were given. Allow your heart to receive the gifts, and journal all that you have experienced. Eat lightly, and drink plenty of water to rehydrate yourself.

◈ Other Journey Explorations

- ◆ Journey to a teacher or power animal to ask, "What is important for me to understand about my first útiseta?" Record the content of your journey and your perceptions about what you received.
- ◆ Journey to ask the spirits of place, "What was your experience of my útiseta ritual?"

After each journey, thank your power animal, your teacher, your shamanic ancestor, and whatever other spirits you meet. Then make an offering outdoors to all the helping spirits.

◈ Process Questions

- ◆ Sing your personal varðlok daily as a part of your personal spiritual practice. Notice how learning your personal varðlok has changed your experience of yourself. Record all that you notice.
- ◆ Check in with yourself for a few months to register any shifts and changes you are feeling from your útiseta. Keep track of what you notice in your journal.
- ◆ How does this útiseta differ from your usual method of shamanic journeying as a method for gaining insight or wisdom? Record your impressions.

13

Performing a
Group Seiðr Ritual

Now you are ready to begin putting all the elements outlined in the previous chapter together. To ensure that you will have a successful ritual, you will need to do the following preparatory work.

To begin, you will need to gather a small group of individuals who can be relied on to support you during the experience. This can be as few as one or two other people that you trust and who have shamanic skills. They should know how to journey and be facile at entering into and returning from the shamanic state of consciousness. There are several reasons to have others present during this. First, when one goes very deeply into trance it is sometimes very difficult to remember the experience once you are back in ordinary reality. Having a witness and even an audio recording of what you share when you are with your teacher or ancestor during the ceremony is a way for you to reexperience the information. Second, support is helpful to assist with drumming and a callback if you don't feel grounded when you return from your journeys. Last, having a friend to share the experience and give you feedback is excellent for improving your skill and helping you to feel safe.

When you have chosen those who will participate, share what you have learned from this book and in your journeys. Teach them the new terminology you have acquired and the skills that you have internalized.

This will help them to better understand what they will be doing and how they can participate.

Once they understand what will be required, teach them the different varðlokur that they will need to know for each of the aspects of the ritual. Since their voices will function in place of your drum or rattle, it is important that they learn the songs well. You may want to share your recordings with them so that they can practice and commit them to memory. Have a few practice sessions so that everyone knows what to do and when to do it!

On the day of the ritual, clear and dedicate the space and gather your materials. A cleared space and time that has been dedicated to spiritual practice is essential to effective results. The time spent doing this is part of your preparation to engage with the spirits. This includes setting up your high seat or seiðhjallr. Although the sagas suggest that the chair was either one especially made for the purpose or a kingly seat that had been raised onto a platform, it can also be an ordinary chair that has been prepared with a special blanket, an animal pelt, or some other way you have received from spirit. When I dedicate a seat for use as a seiðhjallr, I drape a wool blanket that is woven with Viking designs over its surface. The blanket was a special gift and so has a deep meaning for me.

What follows here is the outline of the ritual. Read it completely through to make sure you are clear about how to proceed and practice the elements with your chorus several times to make sure everyone knows the flow.

◈ The Seiðr Ritual

For this exercise, you will need:
- Prepared ritual space, including your high seat or seiðhjallr
- Gathered participants/chorus
- Your seiðr hood and cloak

- Your seiðstafr
- Offering materials
- An audio recorder to capture the information and guidance offered by spirit
- Food and drink for the participants after the ritual
- Your journal or a notebook and pen

◈ Performing the Ritual

As you have done before during the previous exercises, choose a time when you will be able to spend a long, uninterrupted time with the spirits.

Make your offerings outdoors to the spirits even if you are going to be journeying inside. Thank the spirits in advance for their assistance in working with you by making your offering. Take a small bit of your favorite food and place it on the ground. Have your chorus do this with you. Everyone can eat a small bit of this same food in communion with the spirits.

1. Put on your cloak and hood that identifies you as the völva.
2. Take your place in the seiðhjallr, and hold your seiðstafr.
3. Speak the galdr to open the ceremony:
   > Here at the center of all the worlds,
   > Here at the Great Tree, Yggdrasil,
   > We give thanks for fertile Ørlög
   > Through Wyrd, manifesting all things.
   > We hear our ancestors whispering
   > Calling us to remember our power
   > For their descendants yet to be.
4. Sing the varðlok for calling the helpful spirits for the seiðr ritual. The chorus sings this with you.
5. Now call your power animal to you, and merge with the animal. This spirit will protect your spirit body as you journey.
6. Start your audio recording device, and also begin singing your varðlok for entering into the shamanic state of consciousness. The chorus should be singing with you.

7. Place your hood down over your eyes.

8. Once you are in the shamanic state of consciousness, signal an appointed person to ask the question that requires the wisdom of spirit.

9. When you feel ready to access the spirits for the answer, begin singing your journeying/traveling varðlok. The chorus will sing with you.

10. Travel again to Freyja in her guise as the First Shaman.

11. Once you meet Freyja, signal your chorus to begin quietly humming your journeying/traveling varðlok melody. This will allow your journey content and the wisdom of the spirits to be heard by those that are gathered and also to be recorded. From this point forward, narrate all that you experience.

12. Ask Freyja to guide you to the answer. At this point, she will merge with you, ask you to merge with another teacher, or support wisdom to be given in some other way. As with any other journey experience, you will be guided. If at any point you become confused or feel uneasy, refresh your connection with your power animal.

13. During this part of the ritual, the spirits may ask if others have questions or may offer prophecies. Trust the process, and allow it to unfold, but keep aware of your own energy level. End the connection if you start to become fatigued.

14. When the spirits have finished sharing their wisdom, thank them and begin to sing your varðlok of return. This is the song that will bring you back to a present and alert state of awareness. Thank your power animal. Repeat your return varðlok until you feel grounded back in ordinary reality.

15. Remove your hood from your eyes.

Once you feel fully back from your journey, make another offering to all the spirits for their loving assistance.

Close the ritual with a galdr for closure such as:

We honor the Ørlög,

Pregnant with all possibilities.

We honor the Great Tree, Yggdrasil,
And Urð, embodiment of Wyrd.
We honor Freyja the mother shaman,
Our ancestors and helping spirits.
We thank you and release you!

Or this galdr:

Hail Landvaettir and Husvaettir!
Hail our Ancestors!
Hail the Vanir! The Aesir! Our Spirit Teachers!
We honor you all!
Provide us your blessings and protection.
Hail helpful, healing spirits of the Nine Realms!
Go peacefully back to your homes with our gratitude!

Take some time to savor the experience for a while and to understand all that you were given. Allow your heart to receive the gifts, and journal all that you have experienced. Enjoy a meal together, and share with each other what you experienced.

◈ Other Journey Explorations

- Journey to a teacher or power animal to ask, "What is important for me to understand about the seiðr ritual we performed?" Record the content of your journey and your perceptions about what you received.
- Journey to whoever spoke through you or offered wisdom to ask, "What was your experience of the seiðr ritual?"

After each journey, thank your power animal, your teacher, your shamanic ancestor, and whatever other spirits you meet. Then make an offering outdoors to all the helping spirits.

◈ **Process Questions**

- ◆ Decide with your chorus if you want to take turns being the völva in the next seiðr ritual.
- ◆ How does this method of receiving wisdom differ from your usual method of shamanic journeying?
- ◆ Record all of your impressions.

14

The Many Faces of Seiðr

Shamans have always had several functions in their social group. These tasks may be broadly categorized as divinatory, by using spiritual resources to reveal hidden information, and efficacious, by using spiritual resources to create change in the ordinary world. In Viking culture, the seiðr practitioner would have performed tasks ranging from foretelling the future to healing the sick to supporting farms to be fruitful and swaying the outcome of a battle. While I hope you never have to use your spiritual gifts for the latter, there are many more other uses of seiðr that can be easily translated to our twenty-first-century world.

In Viking times, völur would have worked with their helper spirits to accomplish everyday shamanic tasks that assisted in making life easier, helping people and animals in need, creating harmony and balance between the seen and unseen worlds, and participating in preserving social order at the behest of the regional jarl or earl. Neil Price suggests these tasks were typical everyday uses of seiðr:[1]

- Revealing that which is hidden or foretelling the future
- Bestowing blessings or good fortune
- Altering the weather
- Attracting game animals or fish
- Healing the sick
- Communicating and mediating with the dead

- Communicating and mediating with the unseen worlds
- Communicating and mediating with the gods
- Causing mild harm to people, animals, or property

I am not suggesting to you that causing harm be a part of your shamanic repertoire! However, I could imagine that spiritual energies might need to be woven to support those involved in nonviolent protests, which might be considered mildly harmful to the organization, business, or government that is being disrupted by the protest action. The rest of the list can easily be translated for our times into three broader categories: revealing hidden information or performing divination; working with nature and the elemental forces; and functioning as a healer for people, animals, land, or structures.

REVEALING
HIDDEN INFORMATION

Divination is usually thought of as foretelling future events, but the divination done by shamans also involves revealing information that is not only temporally but also spatially hidden from view. For people without helicopters, planes, or other ways to "look ahead," a shaman's journey could have been invaluable in the search for game animals, potable water sources, or safe harbors while sailing uncharted seas. In our world, to be able to see ahead on a physical journey could give you warning of detours or calamities that lie beyond the range of your sight. Such spatial divination can be helpful in finding lost people or animals and assist in finding lost objects or things that were buried beneath the ground, such as objects or structures that were not indicated on a property map.

Reclaiming something lost to the passage of time is another use of divination. This might be used to find an ancient ritual, to reclaim a recipe that was never written down, to access the forgotten history of a place, to learn the name of an ancestor, or how some task was once accomplished.

WORKING WITH
NATURE AND THE ELEMENTS

For our ancestors, the ability to talk with the spirits of nature was vital to their survival. To be able to negotiate with the fish and game animals to have them come closer would have been the difference between starvation and bounty. Working with the elementals to moderate the amount of rain for the crops, asking the harsh winds of a storm to blow higher off the surface of the land to preserve the buildings and trees, and coaxing the sun out to warm the seeds would have also been crucial.

These skills can still be very useful. For instance, I live in a place near a river that is exceptionally prone to lightning strikes. When severe electrical storms are imminent, I go with my helping spirits to meet with the spirit of the storm. I honor the storm's powerful spirit, thank it for its beneficial stirring of the atmosphere, and thank it for its magnificent ability to bring rain. I then ask that it discharge much of its stored energy as cloud-to-cloud lightning instead of connecting with the ground around where there are houses. Once it leaves the land for the ocean, I send it my blessings and thanks.

In the fall, I visit with the spirit of the river before it freezes up. I thank it for the lovely sounds it makes after a rainstorm; the home that it makes for the trout and turtles; as well as the way it carries water to the sea. Then I thank it for being so strong that the snow thaw and spring rains won't breach its banks. I then follow the journeywork with a physical visit to the river to place an offering of cornmeal into the water.

Meeting with the spirits of local animals also provides benefits. Using the ability to communicate with them can mean that it is possible to ask the returning birds what they need in return for their sweet songs or to negotiate with the groundhogs so they don't eat everything in your garden.

FUNCTIONING AS A HEALER

While there is scant evidence in the Icelandic sagas about völur performing healing, it is true that healers employing magical methods were important during the Viking Age. Magical "wise women" were a documented but secretive feature of rural life in Scandinavia well into the nineteenth century and still persist, albeit more openly, today. Indeed, it is impossible for me to think of a shamanic culture that doesn't include some form of healing. Keeping the people in the tribe or longhouse healthy would have been a priority for any shaman and for the Viking völur. As ones who interact with unseen forces, they would be called upon to do battle with illness-causing entities and commune with those spirits who could provide remedies. They would be asked to break the curse of a repetitive pattern of calamity that befell a family, assist in the birthing of children, and aid in the preparation of souls for the afterlife. All of these tasks would have been accomplished by the völva through contacting her helping spirits and ancestors, using the magic words of galdr, and sitting out for guidance, all while keeping her fylgja close for protection.

 Discovering How You Will Use Seiðr

For this exercise, you will need:
- Prepared ritual space including your high seat or seiðhjallr
- Gathered participants/chorus
- Your hood and cloak
- Your seiðstafr
- Offering materials
- An audio recorder to capture the information and guidance offered by spirit
- Food and drink for the participants after the ritual
- Your journal or a notebook and pen

◈ **Making the Discovery**

As before, choose a time when you will be able to spend a long, uninterrupted time with the spirits.

Make your offerings outdoors to the spirits even if you are going to be journeying inside. Thank the spirits in advance for their assistance in working with you by making your offering. Take a small bit of your favorite food and place it on the ground.

1. Put on your cloak and hood that identifies you as the völva, and hold your seiðstafr.
2. Now call your power animal to you, and merge with the animal. This spirit will protect your spirit body on your journey.
3. Begin singing your varðlok for entering into the shamanic state of consciousness. Place your hood down over your eyes.
4. Once you have entered the shamanic state of consciousness, begin singing your journeying/traveling varðlok.
5. Travel again to Freyja in her guise as the First Shaman.
6. Ask Freyja to teach you the ways you are to use seiðr.
7. Once you have learned what Freyja has to share, thank her for her wisdom and begin to sing your varðlok of return—the song that will bring you back to a present and alert state of awareness. Thank your fylgja for her or his protection and love. Repeat your return varðlok until you feel grounded back in ordinary reality.
8. Remove your hood from your eyes.

Once you feel fully back from your journey, make another offering to all the spirits for their loving assistance. You may also wish to speak this galdr:

I honor all that has carried me here.
I honor the Great Tree, Yggdrasil,
And Urð, Embodiment of Wyrd.
I honor Freyja guiding me with her steps,
Working the threads and making harmony.

I thank you all for your wisdom,
And release you with my gratitude!

Take some time to savor the experience for a while and to understand all that you were given. Allow your heart to receive the gifts, and journal all that you have experienced.

◈ Other Journey Explorations

- ◆ Journey to a teacher or power animal to ask, "What is important for me to understand about what I have learned from Freyja?" You may also wish to ask, "How do I keep my practice strong?"
- ◆ Record the content of your journey and your perceptions about what you received.

After each journey, thank your power animal, your teacher, your shamanic ancestor, and whatever other spirits you meet. Then make an offering outdoors to all the helping spirits.

◈ Process Questions

- ◆ What does it mean for you to have these connections and gifts in your life?
- ◆ How do you feel that you are changing as a result of seiðr?
- ◆ Record your impressions, thoughts, and feelings.

15
Learning to See

Meeting with Óðinn

The two families of deities that constitute the Norse/Germanic pantheon may preserve memories of the collision of cultures that began with the severe climate shifts around the fall of Doggerland. The climatic changes that dramatically shifted migration routes of animals and plant species that nourished the hunter-gatherers and proto-agrarian tribes in northern Europe would have made survival in other regions of Eurasia equally difficult.

As temperatures swung widely and regional ecosystems were irrevocably transformed, the pastoralists of western Asia would have had to move into more favorable regions to ensure that their flocks and cultured cereal crops would flourish. Spencer Wells of National Geographic's Genographic Project suggests that beginning approximately 8,000 years ago, people with the R1a1 Y-DNA haplotype* from the southern Asian steppes began their movements westward into Europe.[1]

While we can never be certain of the exact timing of their arrival, the Proto-Indo-European tribes that made their way into the European

---

*Y-DNA is passed father to son and can be used as a tool for studying male population dispersal in the same way that mitochondrial DNA (mtDNA) can trace female genetic dispersal patterns.

continent seemed to have a very different culture from that of the people who had lived there for millennia. Burials of the region discussed earlier in this book suggest that the old European culture was still practicing a female-centric form of shamanism, which included veneration of a Grandmother/Mother Earth archetype, into the Neolithic period. Genetic testing of remains from this period in Scandinavia support this hypothesis. There, bone remains in Neolithic graves indicated that the megalith culture was either matrifocal or matrilineal, as the people buried in the same grave were related through their female lineage.[2] Similar evidence of matrilineal traditions exists among the Picts in northern Britain.

The new arrivals practiced a pantheistic religion that featured a primary male deity, *dyeus ph2tēr* or "sky father." In his book *The Well of Remembrance,* Ralph Metzner postulates that the Æsir family of deities led by the god Óðinn would have been a reflection of the traditions from the east. By the same token, the Vanir more closely reflected the indigenous European worldview.

Indeed, the fact that the Vanir deities' home lies in the western land of the World Tree may preserve an 8,000-year-old memory of the newcomers' westward journey in search of fertile lands. The misty forests and fields of Old Europe must have been a welcome site to those wandering pastoralists from the arid steppes. It must have seemed as though they had entered an extraordinarily alien realm where nature's power was vital and wild. For the people used to open skies and wide horizons, the deep forest must have seemed very strange. Anyone who has traveled into primordial forests can attest to the mysterious nature of that landscape. It is easy to see how the wanderers may have understood that Europe was under the auspices of different spirits!

The newcomers would have called upon their sky god to bring order to their new, unsettling reality. Óðinn represents not only the newcomers' sky god, but epitomizes their desire to understand all that was mysterious, unknown, or challenging. In that way, Óðinn is the personification of the human shaman's role. He wanders creation with his two raven fylgjur to survey what is happening in all the realms. The names of his allies, Huginn (thought) and Munnin (memory), reveal that he is actually sending his consciousness throughout the realms in the guise of the ravens. This is certainly a good description of a shaman's journey!

Óðinn is also known for his eight-legged horse, Sleipnir. Similar horses are seen in shamanic cultures across Siberia as mounts for the shaman as they fly through the realms. Mircea Eliade recounts a Buryat example of an eight-legged foal in his book, *Shamanism: Archaic Techniques of Ecstasy.*

Even with these companions, the newcomers' sky god, Óðinn, wasn't a born shaman like the indigenous Earth Goddess Freyja. Like human beings, this sky deity needed to learn how to be a shaman. For this to occur, he had to transform himself from a western Asian steppe god living in the remote sky to one who walks in all worlds. In that way, Óðinn reflects the adjustments that needed to be made by both the indigenous Europeans and the pastoralist newcomers. Change was necessary, as the old rules no longer applied. His entrance into shamanic mystery is a clear reflection of his people's entrance into unknown territory. He has to learn how to navigate in the darkness of a new and challenging world. In that way, he becomes a role model not only for people entering the shamanic path but also for anyone facing challenging times.

SURRENDERING
THE EGO FOR KNOWLEDGE

In many shamanic cultures, some form of sacrifice is a necessary aspect of initiation for the neophyte shaman. These rituals are as varied as the many shamanic cultures; however, common threads involve a loss or stripping away of the initiate's ordinary way of perceiving reality, as well as a detachment from the personality or ego self. This death and rebirth initiatory experience seems to be a critical aspect of shifting one's understanding of the world from focusing on matter to centering one's thoughts and actions on the spiritual context of life. This loss or moving aside of the obscuring self may be accomplished in several ways. Rituals may include a form of suffering whereby a supplicant is asked

Figure 15.1. This image from the Gotland Picture Stone
depicts Óðinn's eight-legged steed, Sleipnir. This horse's otherworldly
anatomy is related to a similar eight-legged horse that carried
Buryat shamans into the spirit world.

to abstain from food and drink for a prescribed, lengthy period of time, or submit to extreme conditions (heat, cold, wounding) to perceive the death of self in a deep, visionary experience.

Climbing or hanging from a tree is at the center of many shamanic initiatory rights used to achieve a transformation. During these experiences, the shamanic initiate would experience some new view of reality that could include luminous visions, the granting of knowledge, or other spiritual gifts. Óðinn's nine-day period of suffering on the trunk of Yggdrasil, during which he envisions and gathers the runes, certainly parallels this pattern.

The name *Yggdrasil* means "The Terrible One's [Óðinn's] Horse." In other words, the World Tree is Óðinn's vehicle for becoming a shaman. In a shamanic context, Óðinn "dies" in his old life on the tree so that he can be reborn as a visionary. In this case, the World Tree is positioned like the Mother Goddess that generates change.* Like Kali or the tripartite goddess represented by the Norns, who weave and unweave life, the World Tree expunges what interferes with Óðinn's emerging self. He surrenders himself to her to be renewed and reshaped. Yet this initiation is only the beginning of his journey. In grasping the runes Óðinn has only retrieved a parcel of knowledge. He has just opened his eyes. To be able to use the information he has gathered, he must pass other tests to transform his experience into wisdom.

SACRIFICING THE ORDINARY WAY OF SEEING THE WORLD

Taking raw knowledge and forging it into wisdom is a critical task for any shaman. For instance, it isn't enough for an herbal healer to identify medicinal plants or learn how to make a salve. The shaman also needs to discover the nature of illness, determine what medicine the patient requires, know how to administer the dosage, and know how to support the patient to good health. Without these other skills, a neophyte shamanic healer using plants would be no more useful to the patient than a botanical chart.

The runes represent the ability to capture ideas and share magic and the transition from an oral to written culture—in essence the journey from the nonphysical to the physical world. After his ordeal, Óðinn had the letters of a sacred alphabet but did not yet understand how to shape words, poetry, or spells. To gain that ability, he needed to travel down the World Tree to the realm of Urð. It is in the womblike vessel of the Mother Goddess that the promise of Óðinn's complete transformation resides. The water of the well is like the primeval divine female herself. Containing all memory, all wisdom, and the energy of continuance, the water is the vehicle for rebirth.

---

*More about how the World Tree is connected to the Mother Goddess may be found in the next chapter.

Figure 15.2. This rune, known as *fehu*, translates literally as "cattle" and is often associated with the concept of wealth.

The well is guarded by the jötunn Mimir, whose name means "the remember, the wise one" in Old Norse. Remembering is an act that also has parallels in shamanic initiation. During the initial initiatory experience of the neophyte shaman, the candidate may experience a destruction or dissolution of the physical body. In the extreme, this provides an experience of complete formlessness and total detachment from the ordinary life. This spiritual annihilation of the old self is a ritual way for initiates to "die" and then be reborn as a shaman. During the period of dissolution, initiates would be experiencing themselves as a consciousness or spirit bearing witness to the destruction. This would allow a visceral sense of the power of spirit and its ability to move beyond the body. Indeed, this loss of the old body would support initiates to attain a kind of shamanic enlightenment; that is, initiates would be freed to perceive the radiance of spirit that unites all things and beings.

Once the old body is destroyed and the spirit is revealed, the third period begins. This is the subsequent period when the initiate's body is rebuilt by the tutelary spirits. During this remaking or "remembering" experience, there is renewal; however, the initiate's new body is often very different from the one she or he had before the dismemberment.*

In Óðinn's case, he must surrender one of his eyes to drink from the well. This giving up of his ordinary way of seeing gives him a new way of perceiving. A shaman must learn to perceive the world in a very different way from that of an ordinary person. In that role, a person (or in this case, a deity) must learn to navigate through the unseen realms. This is done to find hidden information, to provide insight or guidance, to affect healing, or to look beyond the present time to prophesize the future and resolve the past.

At the point when Óðinn gives up his eye and so some of his ordinary ability/power, he transforms more fully into the role of the shaman. For any contemporary Western aspirant not born into a shamanic culture, this seeker-god provides a model for entering the shamanic path. Not a born shaman, he learns to be one through intention, effort, and sacrifice. In that way, Óðinn's efforts model for us that the shamanic path is attainable by everyone who is willing to undergo a fundamental transformation.

STEPPING INTO BALANCE

To be an effective shaman, one must surrender and allow the spirits to work through you. Often, shamans undergo intentional spiritual possession by tutelary or protector spirits in order to affect change. This act creates a temporary hybrid being that is able to bring the power and wisdom of the unseen realms to the world of physical reality.

For patriarchal tribes, such as the newcomers to Europe and the

---

*See chapter 26 in my book *Spirit Walking: A Course in Shamanic Power* to learn about dismemberment in greater detail.

Vikings of the ninth century, the idea of a man's body being entered by another being may have been unseemly or even taboo.

As Óðinn's story continues to unfold, he learned the art of seiðr from Freyja and so took on a role that had been the exclusive domain of the Vanir. This is quite the step for the powerful masculine god to take. As a result, Óðinn takes a lot of flack from other male Æsir deities. The Icelandic *Ynglingasaga* tells how the god Loki thought magic was unmanly since, "with this sorcery comes such female passion or *ergi* [unmanliness] that it was considered shameful for men to practice, and so the art was taught to the priestesses." In plain language it appears that Loki is calling Óðinn's manhood into question for his choice to practice seiðr. However, Diana L. Paxson suggests that this translation isn't correct. Instead, Loki accuses Óðinn of "*args athal*," which refers to acting in "a sexually receptive way."[3] In other words, like any good shaman, Óðinn was allowing himself to be entered by his helping spirits and allowing his actions to be directed by them.

Óðinn's willingness to expand beyond societal restrictions of roles and gender suggest that this path of transformation can also support a collective evolution. Since he is the chief among the gods in the Norse pantheon, his choice to challenge restrictive gender roles for the benefit of being able to access shamanic magic makes him an excellent guide for our current times. The Old Norse Óðinn* can be considered an antidote to the contrived, hypermasculinized, and cartoonish role models offered to young men by Western culture in the early twenty-first century. His story can support the creation of a new form of healthy masculinity that is not tied to destructive or limitedly rigid patriarchal behaviors.

By taking up the seiðstafr, Óðinn presented a possibility for reconciliation and cultural restructuring. By accepting aspects of the feminine into his life and actions, he was intentionally striding the line between the matricentric and the patriarchal cultures. In interpreting

---

*The Old Norse version of Óðinn is far more complex and has only the flimsiest of connections to the one-dimensional Odin of comic books and movies.

his actions in this way, perhaps one-eyed Óðinn is offering a vision for us in this century. Maybe the message in his story is to surrender our old, outmoded way of seeing. His greatest shamanic act may be to help all of us to see that Western culture's patriarchal behaviors of diminishing women, subjugating other nations, and defiling the environment are both unsustainable and unacceptable.

◈ Meeting Óðinn to Learn to Surrender Unbeneficial Ways of Being

For this exercise, you will need:
- Your preferred method of providing the shamanic journey rhythm
- Your seiðr hood and cloak
- Offering materials
- Some of your favorite food
- Your journal or a notebook and pen
- Your seiðstafr

◈ Making the Journey

As before, choose a time when you will be able to spend a long, uninterrupted time with the spirits. It is best if this work can be accomplished while outdoors. If that is not possible, you may work in a space that you have prepared indoors.

1. Make your offerings outdoors to your helping spirits to thank them in advance for their assistance.
2. Prepare yourself and all the materials as you did in the previous exercises. Once preparations are complete, honor the spirits of all directions, and ask them to bless the area where you will be working.
3. Now call your power animal to you, and merge with the animal. This spirit will protect your spirit body on your journey.
4. Once you have made your offerings and preparations, don your garments and sit in a chair with your seiðstafr.

5. Start your audio recording device, and begin singing your varðlok for entering into the shamanic state of consciousness. Place your hood down over your eyes.

6. Once you have entered the shamanic state of consciousness, begin singing your journeying/traveling varðlok.

7. Travel again to Freyja in her guise as the First Shaman.

8. Ask Freyja to take you to meet Óðinn.

9. Once you meet Óðinn, thank him for agreeing to meet with you.

10. In the presence of Freyja, ask Óðinn to look at you closely and then tell you what aspects of yourself interfere with your growth and evolution as a shamanic practitioner/seiðworker.

11. Ask both Freyja and Óðinn how you may begin to change those unbeneficial aspects.

12. When you have completed your work, thank Óðinn and Freyja for meeting with you and providing their wisdom.

13. Begin to sing your varðlok of return—the song that will bring you back to a present and alert state of awareness. Thank your power animal. Repeat your return varðlok until you feel grounded back in ordinary reality.

14. Remove your hood from your eyes.

Once you feel fully back from your journey, make another offering to all the spirits for their loving assistance.

Take some time to savor the experience for a while and to understand all that you were given. Allow your heart to receive the gifts, and journal all that you have experienced.

A VISION FOR LIFE

Now that you have a better understanding of how to clear away anything that interferes with your spiritual and physical life paths, you can be guided by Óðinn to drink from Urð's well, Urðarbrunnr.

The ritual of drinking from Urð's well, Urðarbrunnr, is an

opportunity to be transformed. Just as knowledge needs to be forged into wisdom, we need to refine our work and evolve as a part of our growth. As shamanic practitioners, we have the privilege of working with remarkable energies and spirits. With this comes the responsibility to work in ways that support the greater whole of Life. In many ways, the path of the shaman in this century requires aspects of spiritual warriorship. Shamans need to keep refining their vision, strengthening their connections to the spirits, and taking spirit-supported actions to bring about harmony and balance in the world.

◈ *Meeting Óðinn to Safely Drink from Urð's Well, Urðarbrunnr*

For this exercise, you will need:
- ◆ Your hood and cloak
- ◆ Offering materials
- ◆ Some of your favorite food
- ◆ Your journal or a notebook and pen
- ◆ Your seiðstafr

◈ Making the Journey

As before, prepare your space and yourself. Then make an offering to the spirits who care for you and protect you.

1. Once preparations are complete, honor the spirits of all directions and ask them to bless the area where you will be working.
2. Now call your power animal to you, and merge with the animal. This spirit will protect your spirit body on your journey.
3. Once you have made your offerings and preparations, don your garments and sit in a chair with your seiðstafr.
4. Start your audio recording device, and begin singing your varðlok for entering into the shamanic state of consciousness. Place your hood down over your eyes.

5. Once you have entered the shamanic state of consciousness, begin singing your journeying/traveling varðlok.

6. Travel again with your power animal to Óðinn.

7. Once you meet him, thank him for agreeing to meet with you.

8. Ask Óðinn to support you to meet with Urð again and to drink safely from Urðarbrunnr.

9. Drink from Urðarbrunnr.

10. When you have completed your work, thank them for meeting with you and providing their wisdom.

11. Begin to sing your varðlok of return, the song that will bring you back to a present and alert state of awareness. Thank your power animal. Repeat singing until you feel grounded back in ordinary reality.

12. Remove your hood from your eyes.

Once you feel fully back from your journey, make another offering to all the spirits for their loving assistance.

Take some time to savor the experience for a while and to understand all that you were given. Allow your heart to receive the gifts, and journal all that you have experienced.

◈ Other Journey Explorations

- ◆ Journey to a teacher or power animal to ask, "In what ways can I continue the evolutionary steps that were suggested by Óðinn?" Record the content of your journey and your perceptions about what you received.

- ◆ Journey to your teachers and power animals to ask each of them, "How do the shifts I make in myself alter the fabric of All That Is?"

- ◆ Journey to your teacher or power animal to ask, "What is the best way to integrate my experience of drinking from Urð's well?"

After each journey, thank your power animal, your teacher, your shamanic ancestor, and whatever other spirits you meet. Then make an offering outdoors to all the helping spirits.

◈ **Process Questions**

- Write down in your journal what it was like to meet with Óðinn.
- What was it like to drink from Urð's well?
- How does it feel to have been given a direction for how to change and evolve?
- How do you feel that you are changing now?
- Record all of your impressions and insights.

16

The Nurturing Tree

The World Tree lies at the intersection of all the realms of existence. It is a "tree of life" symbol in that it unites the human world with the spiritual realms and the world of the deceased ancestors. All the phases of existence and all the possible aspects of reality are held within its roots and branches. This idea is central to the beliefs of northern Eurasian shamans and later Germanic and Scandinavian tribes. However, a cosmic tree can be found in many ancient traditions. Diverse cultures such as the ancient Greeks, Hungarians, Indians, Chinese, Japanese, Persians, Hindus, and ancient Egyptians all understood that a divine tree connected everything that was natural and supernatural. Shamans in the foothills of the Himalayas in Nepal refer to the World Tree as Kalpa Vriksha: the "Tree of Immortality."* An enormous life-sustaining and uniting tree is such a widespread motif in myths and folktales around the world, it can be seen as very nearly universal.[1]

Since the World Tree connects all realities, it is often the way shamans access other realms for their work. During a spirit journey, the World Tree provides a way for the shaman to travel the endless dimensions of spirit while defying the limitations of ordinary time. It is a passage, a portal, and a support that the shaman depends on.

---

*While this tree is upside down—having its roots in the sky and its branches in the lower world—it functions exactly as the World Tree in other cultures.

EVERLASTING, EVERGREEN

The World Tree of the ancient Norse, Yggdrasil, is said to be an ash that is always green. The idea that the World Tree is an ash tree may have its roots in Proto-Indo-European beliefs. This is indicated by the fact that this idea is common to many European cultures, as well as Indian Vedic myths. Vedic shamans would use the branch of an ash tree, which they cut with eight notches, as a ladder into the world of the spirits. The notches represented the seven worlds that they would have to climb through, and the eighth one was the destination. The Sanskrit word for eight is *ash,* so given that names for trees are among the oldest words we have, this suggests that a more ancient Proto-Indo-European language gave us this word.[2]

Many species of ash trees exude a sugary substance that the ancient Greeks called *méli,* a word that means "honey."* This tree honey drips from the ash species, *Fraxinus excelsior,* which grows widely in the forests of Northern Europe. The Norse World Tree, Yggdrasil, is said to "rain honey on the world, and mead is said to flow in its branches,"[3] so it is easy to see how it could be seen as a magical ash tree. This ash honey was used as a food. Even into contemporary times, there were German people and some Scottish Highlanders who provided this substance to newborn babies as their first meal—even before their mother's milk.†

Described as an evergreen, Yggdrasil may also be a yew tree. *Taxus baccata* is an extremely long-lived tree that thrived in Eurasia prior to the Ice Ages.‡ As the glaciers retreated northward, the forests of Europe were over three-quarters yew. The yew is connected to the cycles of life,

---

*The sugary substance secreted by the ash of southern Europe and southwestern Asia (*Fraxinus ornus*) is referred to as *manna.*

†This substance was also fermented into alcohol. Initially, this would have happened naturally in the same way that fallen apples will ferment in the orchard. Later on, this fermentation process would have been developed and refined by humans.

‡All species of yew descended from an ancestor yew (*Paleotaxus rediviva*) that lived over 200 million years ago.

death, and rebirth. Several cultures that predate the Viking Age, including the Celts, Anglo-Saxons, and tribes living in southeastern Europe, viewed the yew as a powerful connector to the ancestors. The wood of the yew is particularly dense and was used for making tool handles, spears, and bows; however, its poisonous nature also made it a dangerous wood to work. Yggdrasil's connection to the yew is suggested by ancient sources that describe it as the "most evergreen tree" (*vetgrønster vida*) and the "needle ash" (*barraskr*). This designation could have been made to overlay the Indo-European's sacred associations of the ash to the already sacred and evergreen yew tree.

No matter the actual species, the World Tree is considered the nourishing and constant center of the cosmos. Paradoxically this unifying force of All Worlds is also a multiplicity. Whenever and wherever shamans prepare an altar or journey to the other worlds, they invoke this center. These many shamans don't work with a representation but rather perceive that the one and only Tree itself is present in their work. This shamanic concept has parallels to the contemporary ideas of physics that suggest that the center of the cosmos is actually everywhere. In this way the unifying center is omnipresent. It is a primordial energy that holds everything that is tangible and intangible—everywhere, all at once. This is quite fitting, as the World Tree also has many connections to the Mother Goddess.

HOLDING ALL THE WORLDS

In holding all of creation, the Tree of Life personified the female principle. Edwin Oliver James, in his book *Tree of Life: An Archaeological Study*, suggests that, during the time farming first arose in the Neolithic the female principle was still in predominance. In western Asia, the Aegean, and Crete a sacred tree was primarily the embodiment of the Goddess, often in association with her young, virile male partner as husband, son, and lover. By the time of the Middle Minoan period, the Goddess began to emerge as an individualized anthropomorphic figure in her threefold capacity of the Earth Mother, the Mountain Mother or Sky Goddess, and Underworld or Death Goddess. As the Tree of Life took human form it became in due course the Great Mother of many names, who was the personification of the female principle in all its life-giving aspects. The female nature of the World Tree became fixed in human imagination.[4]

Preserved into the twentieth century, the stories of the Nenet, Enet, Nganasan, and Selkup tribes of Siberia,* honor the World Tree in its usual place as the connector of different realities. However, their mythologies also describe it as the symbol of Mother Earth, who is said to have given the drum to the First Shaman and to assist all shamans' travels from one world to the other. These are the same roles that have been assigned to the Mother Goddess/First Shaman.

Even in the Judeo-Christian Old Testament, trees are also associated with the ancient Canaanite religion devoted to the Mother Goddess, Asherah. She is the goddess whose veneration the Israelites sought to suppress and replace with their god, Yahweh. The Goddess Asherah and her consort Baal were honored on the tops of hills and mountains, where carved wooden poles or statues of the goddess were placed.[5] The name *Asherah* has also been translated to mean "grove, wood, or tree."

THE MOTHER TREE CREATRIX

Further evidence that the World Tree is another symbol for the primordial goddess is the World Tree's role in the creation or emergence of human beings on the Earth. According to Anders Hultgård of Uppsala University, the people who descended from early Proto-Indo-Europeans have myth structures that place the origin of humankind either from trees or from wood.[6] However, this creation story is not limited to these cultures. Native people near my home in North America—the

---

*These peoples are all members of the Samoyedic language group that once also included the Yurats, Kamasins (or Kamas), Khakas, Karagass, Taygi, and Mator tribes.

Passamaquoddy, Penobscot, Mi'kmaq, and Maliseet tribes of Maine and eastern Canada—share an origin myth of their ancestors emerging from an ash tree.[7] In fact, trees are important as sources of creation for diverse cultures, including the Maasai in Africa, the Oceanic peoples of the Banks Islands, the Indonesian Dyaks, and native people of Papua New Guinea, as well as the Acoma people of southwestern America.[8]

Norse myths have two stories of people either being created from or emerging from inside trees. Ask, the first man, and Embla, the first woman, were created from trees. Ask's name is a derivative of the Old Norse word *askr,* which means "ash tree." According to Benjamin Thorpe, "the word *embla, emla,* signifies a busy woman, from *amr, ambr, aml, ambl, assiduous labour.* . . ."[9] However, the name may have derived from a word meaning "vine." Vine is a soft wood that can be used as a flammable base for the drill used to kindle a fire. Embla's name can therefore have two connotations. Indo-European cultures equate the action of kindling a fire in this manner with sexual inter-course; however, the other analogy may simply suggest the more ancient idea that the feminine aspect brings forth life-giving light and heat to the world. In this sense, Embla is born from the tree and becomes the ember that ignites the human race.

The second Norse story of trees and humans is set during the end of the world. In Norse myth, the reign of the gods ends in a spectacular cataclysm called Ragnarök. During this time, all the worlds and gods are destroyed. However, one deity, Freyja, and two people survive the end of all things. The woman, Lif (Life),* and man, Lifthrasir ("Life's lover" or "Zest for Life"), survive by taking shelter in the great tree. There they sleep through the destruction of the worlds, and when they awaken, they find that the Earth is green and verdant again. It is suggested that the magical couple will become the progenitors of a new race of humans, and their descendants will inhabit the renewed world.

---

*The name *Lif* is identical with the Old Norse feminine noun meaning "life, the life of the body."

THE WORLD TREE AS WOMB

Having the role as shelter and place of rebirth for Lif and Lifthrasir, the tree holds a womblike parallel to the caves that our early ancestors venerated. Entering the painted caves of the Paleolithic required that our ancestors squeeze themselves into the dark belly of the Earth. Often, these passages were covered in red ochre resembling birthing blood. It is in these uterus-like chambers that the ancestors painted their extraordinary images of animals. Perhaps these paintings were a way to shamanically implant the spirits of animals in the womb of the Earth Mother so that they could be born into this world. This idea certainly has comparisons to other shamanic rituals that are designed to influence the moment of manifestation when the spiritual becomes physical.

In addition, the World Tree unites all realities. Connecting the Earth to both the heavens above and the underworld below, it is the passageway through which a shaman travels. In this way the story of Lif and Lifthrasir suggests that rebirth may be achievable through entering the tree or behaving as shamans do, the implication being that by remembering our oldest way of understanding our world, we can help to renew it for the future.

◈ *Entering the Regenerative Womb of the World Tree*

For this exercise, you will need:

- ◆ Your preferred method of providing the shamanic journey rhythm
- ◆ Your seiðr hood and cloak
- ◆ Offering materials
- ◆ Some of your favorite food
- ◆ Your journal or a notebook and pen
- ◆ Your seiðstafr

◈ Making the Journey

1. As you have done before, make all of your usual journey preparations. Once preparations are complete, honor the spirits of all directions, and ask them to bless the area where you will be working.
2. Now call your power animal to you, and merge with the animal. This spirit will protect your spirit body on your journey.
3. Once you have made your offerings and preparations, don your hood and sit in a chair with your seiðstafr.
4. Start your audio recording device, and begin singing your varðlok for entering into the shamanic state of consciousness. Place your hood down over your eyes.
5. Once you have entered the shamanic state of consciousness, begin singing your journeying/traveling varðlok.
6. Travel again to Freyja, the First Shaman.
7. Ask Freyja to assist you to enter the regenerative womb of the World Tree.
8. Once you enter the Womb of Regeneration, begin to softly sing your personal power song.
9. Notice the sensations and emotional feeling you have in this place.
10. When you feel complete, thank Freyja and the World Tree/Goddess.
11. Begin singing your varðlok of return, and continue to sing it until you are fully back in ordinary reality.
12. Remove your hood from your eyes.

Once you feel fully back from your journey, make another offering to all the spirits for their loving assistance. Take some time to savor the experience for a while and to understand all that you were given. Allow your heart to receive the gifts, and journal all that you have experienced.

◈ Other Journey Explorations

- Journey to a teacher or power animal to ask, "Show me what happened to me while I was inside of the womb of the World Tree." Record the content of your journey and your perceptions about what you received.

- Journey to ask, "How can I continue my transformation?"
- Journey to your teachers and power animals to ask each of them, "What is my part in helping to renew the Earth?"

After each journey, thank your power animal, your teacher, your shamanic ancestor, and whatever other spirits you meet. Then make an offering outdoors to all the helping spirits.

◈ **Process Questions**
- Write down in your journal what it was like to be inside of the regenerative womb of the World Tree.
- Reflect on how your changes benefit the whole.

TUNTRE/VÅRDTRÄD: HONORING YOUR OWN SACRED TREE

People all over Scandinavia once planted or consecrated special trees in their yards and on their farms. These trees, known as a *tuntre* in Norwegian or a *vårdträd* in Swedish, served as a constant reminder of the sacredness of place. These trees provided connections to the ancestors who once lived on the land and to the nature spirits that kept the area safe and fertile. These trees were seen as "local representatives" of sacred groves, bringing the wild and powerful connections to the spirits into a more domesticated setting. They also provided a place to make offerings, to pray, to honor the spirits, and to contact the ancestors. These trees were thought of as so sacred that no one would cut or wound one of them in any way. The health of these special trees was of paramount importance because of the belief that, should the tree sustain some injury, a misfortune would befall the residents of the property. The connection between these individual trees and the wider world of the spirits was explicit. In a larger sense, these specially honored trees were perceived as stand-ins for the World Tree, Yggdrasil.

In some cases, entire villages would have a sacred, guardian tree, which was situated in the center of the town. This tuntre/vårdträd metaphorically united the town with its roots and sheltered the area from harm with its branches. Whether situated in the town center or on a local farm, each of these special trees was cared for and honored by those people who lived with them.

Most of these sacred trees were long-lived varieties that would last for many generations. If they were deciduous trees they might be varieties such as oak, ash, maple, and linden. If a conifer, it would be a Norway spruce or other evergreen that would last for many generations. There is a 9,550-year-old Norway spruce named "Old Tjikko" living in the Fulufjället Mountains of Sweden. It is the oldest single-stemmed clonal tree and originally took root not long after the glaciers retreated from Scandinavia. It has been confirmed as the planet's longest-lived

Figure 16.1. The Norway spruce is an example of the type of sacred guardian tree that might have been found throughout Scandinavia.

plant identified so far, even surpassing the venerable elder bristlecone pines of the western United States.[10]

This tradition of venerating places on the land with trees began in the pre-Christian Viking Age in Scandinavia, but I suspect the practice has much older, shamanic roots. Trees are consecrated and honored in many shamanic traditions—especially across Central Siberia's taiga forest. These trees were thought of as places to interact with the Master Spirits of animals and birds, provided a seat for the guardian spirits of the land, and were a place where the ancestors were honored.* Offerings were placed in and around these trees, and prayers were made in and around their branches as they functioned as transmitters that were capable of transporting the peoples' messages directly to the spirits. In other words, they function as portals for us into the realm of spirit.

The tradition of having a tuntre/vårdträd remained a vibrant tradition in Scandinavia until fairly recently, yet just as the custom was in jeopardy of being lost to time, it is beginning to see a resurgence of interest. Certainly, now is an excellent time to renew interest in the spirits of the land and to once again develop deep relationships with the natural world.

The Norwegian phrase *"Kjennskap gir Vennskap"* refers to the kind of knowledge one gains by taking an active, participatory role in life. It is the deep wisdom of life experience that comes from using all of your senses to taste, touch, see, and hear the world around you. By specifically immersing yourself in nature and learning how she works, you develop a feeling of deep kinship with her. From that sense of kinship springs a love and awareness to protect her. That feeling then kindles a profound desire to take thoughtful, informed action on nature's behalf.

Having your own local representative of Yggdrasil can be one way for you to participate with the spirits of place and your ancestors, too.

---

*A wonderful selection of color photos of these specially honored trees from Tuva, Mongolia, and around Lake Baikal were used to accompany my article, "So the Spirits Feel Treasured" in *Sacred Hoop Magazine*, 2014, no. 85: 14–19.

◈ *Dedicating a Sacred Tree on or near Your Land*

Begin this process by looking in and around where you live to find a likely candidate for your tuntre/vårdträd. It may be a venerable old tree in good health, a tree that is planted in an auspicious place such as near your door, one that is especially beautiful, or a tree that holds important memories for you.

Before you enter into a spiritual relationship, find out a bit about the tree. Find out the answers to a few simple ordinary reality questions, such as what species is the tree? Is the tree native to your region? What kind of care does the tree need to stay healthy? These are all questions that can be answered by the experts you might find at your local cooperative extension or Audubon center. Once you have a better sense of who your tree is, then you can follow these steps to dedicate it for sacred purpose.

For this exercise, you will need:
- ◆ Your preferred method of providing the shamanic journey rhythm
- ◆ Your seiðr hood and cloak
- ◆ Offering materials
- ◆ Some of your favorite food
- ◆ Your journal or a notebook and pen
- ◆ Your seiðstafr
- ◆ A recording device to capture the tree's varðlok

◈ Making the Journey

1. Make all of your usual journey preparations. Once they are complete, honor the spirits of all directions, and ask them to bless the area where you will be working.
2. Now call your power animal to you, and merge with the animal. This spirit will protect your spirit body on your journey.
3. Once you have made your offerings and preparations, don your hood and sit with the tree.

4. Start your audio recording device, and begin singing your varðlok for entering into the shamanic state of consciousness. Place your hood down over your eyes.

5. Once you have entered the shamanic state of consciousness, begin singing your journeying/traveling varðlok.

6. Have your fylgja take you to meet with the spirit of the tree.

7. Upon meeting the tree, introduce yourself.

8. As a part of your introduction, begin to softly sing your personal varðlok or power song.

9. After a few moments of singing, ask the tree to sing her or his varðlok to you.

10. Learn the song so that you can sing it back to the tree anytime.

11. Ask the tree what it needs from you in return for becoming a spiritual center in your life.

12. Thank the tree for its willingness to be a part of your life.

13. When you feel complete, begin singing your varðlok of return and continue to sing it until you are fully back in ordinary reality.

14. Remove your hood from your eyes.

Once you feel fully back from your journey, make another offering to all the spirits for their loving assistance, and make an offering to the tree as well. Take some time to savor the experience for a while and to understand all that you were given. Allow your heart to receive the gifts, and journal all that you have experienced.

◈ Other Journey Explorations

- Journey to a teacher or power animal to ask, "Show me how I am connected to this tree." Record the content of your journey and your perceptions about what you received.
- Journey to ask, "How can I honor this tree?"
- Journey to your teachers and power animals to ask each of them, "How is my relationship with this tree connected to the renewal of the Earth?"

After each journey, thank your power animal, your teacher, your shamanic ancestor, and whatever other spirits you meet. Then make an offering outdoors to all the helping spirits.

◈ **Process Questions**
- Write down in your journal what it was like to sing and be sung to by your tuntre/vårdträd.
- Reflect on how the changes you are making in your life contribute to benefiting the whole.

CONCLUSION

Ragnarök or Renewal?

In the Norse myths, Ragnarök is foretold as the time when all the worlds of the gods and humans are destroyed in a series of disasters triggered as a result of the foolish actions of warring gods. All the realms fall into darkness, the worlds of gods and humans burn, and the seas swallow the land.

Our ancestors had to endure tremendous climatic changes that involved the destruction of land and the familiar ways of life they supported. Today, we are facing a similar cataclysm, only this time on a global scale. Great changes in the climate are changing weather patterns and in turn negatively affecting ecosystems, food production, and health. Rising sea levels jeopardize global coastlines and the enormous numbers of people who live there. This time it isn't the ending of an ice age or other natural disaster that is disrupting our way of life and threatening the future of all species. This time, we are facing a life-ending cataclysm or Ragnarök of our own creation.

We have been brought here by the tyranny of patriarchal culture. This ideology has created a small group of individuals and corporations who have sought to control wealth and power at the expense of the natural world, other species, women, children, and the majority of men as well. It is a social structure with a fear of loss at its foundation. This fear generates a desire for wealth and power at the expense of other beings, cultures, and the environment. So what can we do to preserve the biosphere and all the beings who inhabit it?

There is an Old Norse word that can give us a clue. The word is *hamingja*, which means two things. First, the word means the personification of the good fortune or luck of an individual or family. Hamingja also means the altered appearance of a shapeshifter. Since it refers to shape-shifting, the word is closely connected to the shamanic concept of power animals or fylgjur.

This is interesting that changing shape and luck are intimately woven into one word. This idea suggests to me that good fortune is possible through our personal transformation. In addition, it may be that remembering and bringing forth the sacred feminine for all people is key. According to Norse myths, the sudden appearance of a fylgja can portend a death. This seems to correlate well in that the upsurge of interest in shamanism is happening at precisely this time that is so perilous for both our species and our planet. It is clear that our catastrophic way of relating to the planet, other species, and one another must die away—the death foreshadowed by the fylgja, or need for change. In addition, the myths go on to say that when fylgjur appear in the feminine form they are seen as guardian spirits or preservers.

Since our destructive culture is a reflection of the conflicts that exist inside us, we need to transform ourselves and, in so doing, our patriarchal culture to correct our destructive trajectory.

First, it means learning to live in the way the powerful shamans of the past have lived; that is, to work in harmony and stay in communication with the other beings around us. We can do this through journeying, ritual, and respectful interactions. We human beings need to remember that we are intimately connected to all beings. We cannot live without healthy ecosystems. All that is necessary for our survival exists on this one tiny world floating in the vast, cold vacuum of space. This is the only home that our species knows. We have nowhere to run or hide. No amount of money or power will save us from the demise of our planet. We need to work in harmony with her, *now*.

Second, we need to intentionally return sacred feminine to the forefront. Not to supplant men but to stand shoulder to shoulder with each other to heal the wounds created through a little over six centuries of patriarchal culture.

Anthropological evidence suggests that most prehistoric hunter-gatherer societies were relatively egalitarian, and that patriarchal social structures did not develop until many years later, following social and technological innovations such as agriculture and domestication of animals. Agrarian lifestyles depend on controlling good arable or grazing land and also promote the need to control other resources such as water. This gives birth to ideas of ownership that differ from the sharing lifestyle of hunter-gatherers. The ideas of "mine/yours" and "us/them" developed into the creation of "haves and have-nots." Patriarchy promotes success through domination rather than cooperation and creates a small powerful class that controls the larger population. This in turn creates scenarios in which those in the dominated group seek to gain status by fighting other members of the same strata. The dominant group encourages this behavior so that the larger populace remains disjointed and so incapable of overthrowing those who are oppressing them.

Jungian psychology perceives patriarchy as an expression of a stunted, immature form of masculinity and thus as an attack on masculinity in its fullness, as well as on femininity in its fullness. To save our world, our immaturity must end. To change our dire situation, we need to each bring forth our individual brilliance and work collectively. To do this we need to rid ourselves of the poisons of division. We do this by working with shamanic methods of journeying, ritual, and communion with nature to heal the places in ourselves that hold on to weakness, jealousy, powerlessness, greed, fear, and anger. In turn, this will help us to transform not only our destructive Western culture but also the entire human collective.

As we heal, we then must reenter into a harmonious relationship with the natural world. When we remember that humans and all other species are one family—one large, interconnected organism—then we can pull together to take back our planet from those people, industries, and corporations that are destroying all that we need to survive. After

Figure 17.1. We can use our intrinsic power in two very different ways.
One is to follow our current path of environmental degradation, and the
other is to turn ourselves around and work together, like these
interwoven dragons, toward planetary renewal.

all, we as a species are hybrids of older and newer versions of us. We
spread across the globe and in that process each small group of us held
on to truths from our past and garnered new ideas. We intermingled
some of our cultural wisdom even as some was lost. Imagine what we
could accomplish if we begin to see ourselves as one large organism that
has assimilated into itself a wealth of individual pieces of a great puzzle;
we can come together to share those pieces to create a whole picture of
us and our world.

The American astronomer, astrophysicist, cosmologist, author, and
science communicator Carl Sagan suggested that we have accumulated
dangerous evolutionary baggage on our journey through time. As part of
this baggage, he recalled our propensities for aggression, our willingness

to submit to leaders so we might "feel safe," and our hostility to those we consider "outsiders." These are traits that have put our survival in some doubt. On the other hand, he observed our ability to acquire passion for others and to love our children, a desire to learn from experience, and the soaring and passionate intelligence we have refilled over many millennia. While Sagan believed we have the clear tools for our continued survival and prosperity, he found it unclear which of the aspects of our nature would prevail.

What is certain is that if we continue the path we are on or choose to do nothing, our fate and the fate of all other species on our world are sealed. It is time to take up the drum, to dance with the Earth Mother, and enter the World Tree. We need to relearn the heart and soul of who we are. In relearning our true power as radiant beings of enormous power, we can unleash our collective genius and merge our collected wisdom to develop strategies for healing what we have done in our ignorance and arrogance. It is how we can emerge as many versions of Lif and Lifthrasir. We can become the new humans who will contribute in bringing forth a verdant new world.

An Introduction to Shamanic Journeying

The shamanic journey is a method for exploring hidden realms beyond the limits of our senses and our ordinary perceptions of time and space. The journey functions as a bridge between our everyday state of awareness and an expanded state that provides access to deeper worlds of consciousness, which hold the wisdom of Nature, of the ancestors, and of transcendent spirit beings. Practiced by people for tens of thousands of years, it is based on the understanding that everything has a spirit or consciousness that can be available for communication and relationship.

In the journey state, our brain emits waves in the high alpha/theta range, and activity shifts more into the right hemisphere. During this process our imagination is heightened, as is our intuition, creativity, and ability to problem solve and synthesize information. With continued practice, these beneficial effects also become more sustained even while in ordinary awareness.

The journey through a spiritual landscape provides a kind of interface for the mind to assimilate information, guidance, and insight from the numinous world. The familiar reference of "place" supports that which lies beyond our senses—the nonlocal world—to be more easily grasped. These hidden realms are typically perceived as having three levels.

The Lower World is a realm beneath the earth that is characterized by lush and vibrant landscape. It is filled with the spirits of animals, rocks, birds, plants, and those creatures that are extinct or that we think of as mythological. The Lower World feels very primordial in nature. For instance, an animal in the Lower World feels more like an ancestor or spiritual template for the physical animals that live on Earth.

Passing through the sky accesses the Upper World. Many kinds of spirits are found in this level. The spiritual teachers found in the Upper World make themselves available to answer our questions, guide our steps, and encourage our own inherent inner wisdom. Like Lower World spirits, these teachers are safe sources of knowledge. These spirits, who have no need for a form, take a shape that is most useful for our interactions, which is most often humanlike in appearance.

The hidden reality of the world in which we live is called the Middle World. This place is inhabited by all the spirits of the natural world, the elements as well as the guardian spirits of nature we call "the Hidden Folk." The nisse, elves, dwarves, trolls, faeries, sprites, and other similar beings are those who were honored by our ancestors as protectors and enliveners of the natural world.

Middle World is also the place of physical manifestation. It is the place where the word is made flesh, where quantum vibration becomes physical matter. This refers not only to living beings but also the energies of feelings, thoughts, and desires. For this reason, we need to be able to work both safely and with humility in this realm. The Middle World is where, in our unconsciousness, human beings have manifested the unbeneficial energies that need to be rebalanced. It is also where the disembodied spirits of the dead, negative emotional energy, and other spiritual and physical hazards reside.

While the Middle World is rich with spiritual wisdom, journeyers need to learn to do this safely and with discernment. For these reasons, it is necessary to make strong connections with protective, helpful, and healing spirits in the Lower and Upper Worlds before doing more work in the Middle World.

Journeys are accomplished by using repetitive rhythms that assist us to more easily enter a visionary state. These may include stimuli such as repetitive drumming, rattling, chanting, or dancing. It is also useful to close off or diminish our ordinary sight with a blindfold or other screen so that our inner vision or "strong eye" can become more prominent.

A guardian spirit in the form of an animal or bird (the Norse fylgja) typically accompanies a journeyer on their visionary excursion. These guardians are called power animals. A power animal is different from the animal spirits of the Middle World, being a transcendent spirit that is a teacher, guide, protector, and companion for the shaman. These spirits remind us of a primordial time when people and animals were more closely connected. In her essay, "Rock Art and the Material Culture of Siberian and Central Asian Shamanism," Ekaterina Devlet explained that many Siberian tribes believe that in the mythical, timeless period before the remembered time of human beings (a concept somewhat akin to the so-called Dreamtime of Australian aborigines) there were no distinctions in form or essence between people, animals, and birds. Furthermore, there is also a common belief throughout Siberia that when shamans step outside of ordinary time and space to enter into the timeless world of the spirits, it gives them access to this deep, ancient kinship bond.

During the journey, a shaman receives information and guidance and then retraces her steps to return fully to ordinary consciousness. This moving in and out of this visionary state is what defines the shaman.

Here are the directions to have you do a journey to meet a power animal or fylgja. Your journey will begin in a favorite place in nature and go into the Lower World.

◈ *Journey to Meet a Power Animal, or Fylgja*

For this exercise, you will need:

- ◆ A comfortable place to sit or lie down
- ◆ A way to listen to the shamanic journey rhythm (A free download of a 15-minute journey drumming audio track with callback signal can be found at www.evelynrysdyk.com/myspiritwalk.html)

- ◆ A blindfold or bandana for covering your eyes
- ◆ Your journal or a notebook and pen

◈ Making the Journey

1. First, situate yourself in your comfortable place and in a comfortable position with your blindfold over your eyes.
2. Put on the headphones and have the recording ready to play, but do not start it yet. This recording will help you to expand your awareness into the journey state more easily.
3. Take a few minutes to breathe deeply and remember something that fills you with gratitude.
4. Once you have gotten yourself fully into gratitude, allow your memory to take you back to the most magical of your place memories. Choose a place in which you have felt safe. These are often places in nature we have felt to be sacred. Once in that place in your memory, allow yourself to reexperience it with all of your senses.
5. Filled with the strong feelings of your place, begin the shamanic journey drumming audio file. While listening to the drumming, engage all of your senses in "being" in your special place. Notice as much as you can. What time of day is it? Where is the sun or moon? Is there a breeze or is it still? Are there the scents of flowers, the ocean, or pine trees? What is the ground around you like? Be as fully present in this place as you are able. Continue to explore. Get to know the trees, stones, and plants of your power-filled place.
6. Look for a place where you can go down to the Lower World. This can be an animal burrow, a hollow tree, or some other opening in the Earth.
7. Enter the opening with the intention to travel downward into the Lower World to meet your fylgja.
8. Keep going down through the passageway until you come out in a landscape.
9. Continue to repeat your heart's intention about meeting the spirit of your power animal. Feel it already accomplished, and while doing so, use all of your senses to look for an animal or bird that is revealing itself to you.
10. You will know when you meet a power animal by noticing an animal or

bird that stays close. The animal may greet you, speak to you, or make some other strong form of connection. Be persistent until you meet.

11. Continue getting to know your power animal until the drumming changes to the callback signal.

12. Once you hear the change in the drumming, thank the power animal for being with you and retrace your steps back to your starting place. As you retrace your steps, you will return your awareness to ordinary reality.

13. When the callback is finished, take a deep breath, gently remove your headphones and blindfold, and open your eyes.

Take some time to savor the experience for a while and to understand all that you were given. Allow your heart to receive the gifts, and journal all that you have experienced.

◈ Journey Explorations

- ◆ Journey to your fylgja to ask, "How do I honor you?" Record the content of your journey and your perceptions about what you received.
- ◆ Journey to your fylgja to ask, "How can you help me in my life?"
- ◆ Journey to your fylgja to ask, "How may we work together in harmony?"

If you didn't meet a power animal/fylgja initially, don't worry, as this kind of work can take some time. Be persistent, and keep journeying to the Lower World until you do. Indeed, once you meet this being, you'll want to make numerous journeys to it. You are in the process of developing a power-filled relationship, so each of you must get to know the other. Let your power animal show you around the Lower World. Get to know how it communicates with you and how you are able to understand each other. Be compassionate and gentle with yourself as you learn, and practice journeying to your power animal until you feel truly connected with this wonderful being!

◎ ◎ ◎

There are many methods available to you to learn more about the shamanic journey process. There are several recommended books, audios, and teachers in the resources section at the back of this book.

APPENDIX B

Making
a Seiðr Hood

As stated earlier in this book, the seiðr hood is not only a badge of office, it is an empowered ally or gandr that accompanies and assists the seiðkona or seiðmaðr during the shamanic ritual. A hood and cloak were common garments during the medieval period and were worn across Eurasia. The hood functions not only to cover the head but also to provide an extra layer of protection to the shoulders. This would have been especially important in the damp and cold weather of Scandinavia. It is also very useful to keep one more comfortable during an útiseta wilderness quest.

During the seiðr ritual, the hood can function as a mask to shield the eyes, which can make the alteration of consciousness easier. Pulled down in that fashion, it also has the effect of altering the voice of the wearer so that it has a somewhat disembodied quality. This helps to heighten the effect of the spoken words on those gathered for the ritual.

Making your own shamanic gear is something that I suggest to my students. However, if you aren't comfortable with sewing fabric, I recommend that you work together with a friend who has that skill. The important thing is to be as engaged in the process as is possible for you so that you have a different relationship with the completed hood as your personal shamanic tool. Be sure to read through all of the directions before you begin the project.

CHOOSING FABRIC

I recommend that if you will be primarily using your hood indoors, you keep it as lightweight as you can while retaining its opaqueness as an eye covering. In Viking times, wool and linen were the most common fabrics, and both of these would make good hood choices. If you will be using your hood outdoors I recommend using heavier-weight wool. The directions that follow are for a traditional unlined hood. If you wish to have a lining, a person skilled in sewing can help to translate these instructions to create one.

Traditional colors used in Viking times include various browns, golden yellows, rust and orange, pale blues, navy blue, various greens, deep burgundy reds, light gray, and charcoal gray. I prefer a dark fabric as it helps the hood to be more opaque, but use whatever color feels right and heightens your connection with your spirits.

MAKING THE HOOD

Whatever fabric you choose, be sure to wash and dry it first so that it is preshrunk and any chemical treatments or extra dye is removed. Then iron the fabric under a damp cloth to preserve the nap before trying to cut pieces out for your hood. Flat fabric is a must to make sure your cuts are even and straight.

The instructions that follow are for recreating a Viking hood from a 995–1029 CE bog burial in Skjoldehamn on the island of Andøya. This is the northernmost island in the Vesterålen archipelago that lies inside the Arctic Circle in Norway. The person wearing this hood was a small-statured person, which could have suggested the person was Sami. Instead, DNA analysis determined that she was a Viking Age woman with no Sami ancestry who was wearing a Sami-influenced tunic and trousers usually reserved for males! (When a burial confuses the archaeologists, I always wonder if it indicates a shaman!)

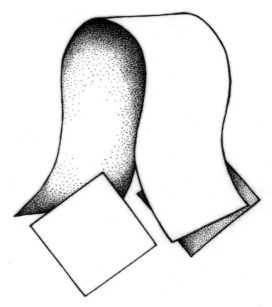

Figure B.1. This is the way the pieces of the hood will fit together.
The sewing is done with the right side of the fabric inside,
which is shaded in this illustration.

◈ *Sewing Instructions*

1. You will be cutting three pieces total from your fabric. One long piece that is 16½ inches wide by 54 inches long, and two smaller pieces that are 12½ inches square. Since fabric is sold in various widths, make sure you will be able to get all the pieces that you need from your fabric.

2. Align your pieces so that they are parallel to the selvage edge of the fabric.

3. You may sew the pieces of the fabric together by hand or by machine. As Viking garments were very well and finely constructed, use small, closely placed stitches.

4. Following the layout shown in figure B.2, sew the front panel to the long piece with the right/finished side of the two pieces of fabric together. Use a ½-inch seam allowance. Stop the seam about ½ inch from the top edge of the small piece, and secure the thread.

5. Then sew the second smaller panel as indicated. Press the seams flat.

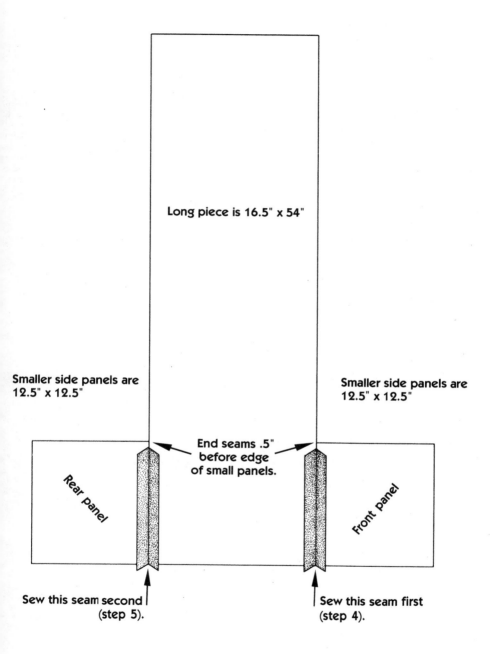

Figure B.2. This illustration indicates the
first two seams you will sew.

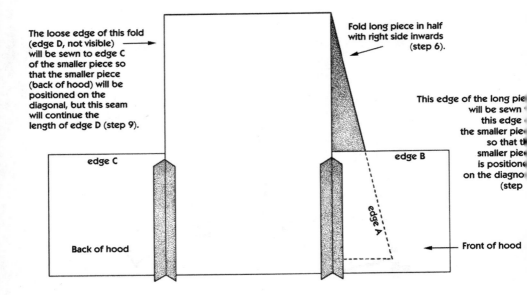

The loose edge of this fold (edge D, not visible) → will be sewn to edge C of the smaller piece so that the smaller piece (back of hood) will be positioned on the diagonal, but this seam will continue the length of edge D (step 9).

Fold long piece in half with right side inwards (step 6).

This edge of the long piece will be sewn to this edge of the smaller piece so that the smaller piece is positioned on the diagonal (step

edge C

edge B

edge A

Back of hood

Front of hood

Figure B.3. Fold down the long piece so that the right side of the fabric is inside of the fold.

6. Next, fold the long piece in half with the right side of the fabric inside.

7. Pin together lower edge A of the long piece to the smaller front panel edge B so that the smaller front panel edge B is on the diagonal (figures B.3 and B.4). This step forms the hood opening.

8. Sew edge B of the smaller front panel to edge A of the folded long piece. As before, end the seam ½ inch before the edge. You will have a little tab of unsewn fabric at the neckline. Press the seams flat (figure B.4).

9. To close the hood back, pin edge C to edge D, creating what will become the long seam of the back of the hood (figure B.5). Start sewing from the bottom of edge C and edge D up to the folded edge of the long piece, attaching the top edge of the rear panel short seam as you sew. Press seams flat.

10. Once all the seams are done, fold down that tab of fabric at the neck and sew it in place (figure B.6).

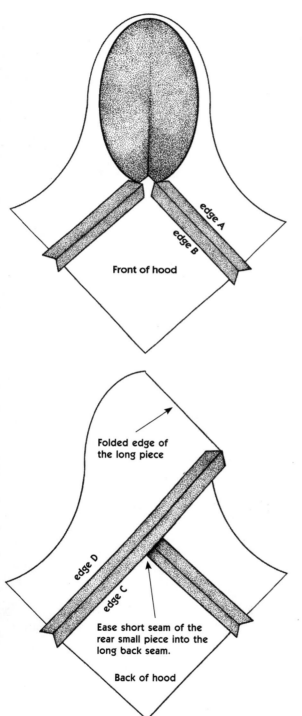

Front of hood

edge A

edge B

Figure B.4. Once the second side of the front panel is secured; there will be a tab at the front of the hood opening left unsewn.

Folded edge of the long piece

edge D

edge C

Ease short seam of the rear small piece into the long back seam.

Back of hood

Figure B.5. The long seam runs from the bottom edge all the way to the fold and catches the top of the short seam.

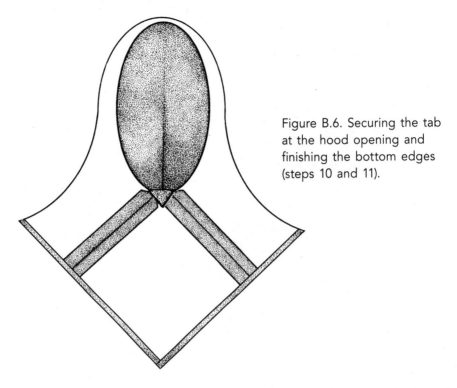

Figure B.6. Securing the tab at the hood opening and finishing the bottom edges (steps 10 and 11).

11. Then fold the bottom edges of the hood twice and secure with a line of stitches to make a finished bottom edge.
12. Once these steps are complete, turn your hood so that the right side of the fabric faces outward.

SURFACE DECORATION

At this point you can add traditional Viking Age surface decoration stitches to finish the hood. To remain authentic, these stitches can be done with either unwaxed linen thread in white, buff, or an unbleached color or in tapestry wool in a color that accents your hood fabric. If being strictly authentic isn't a concern, use ordinary embroidery thread—three strands at a time. The bottom edge and around the hood can be finished with blanket stitches or decorated with traditional herringbone stitches. I have included diagrams of the blanket stitch and three traditional variations on the herringbone stitch. For making a line-work design, you may want to use the split stitch that is also shown below.

Try practicing them on scraps of your hood fabric first so you are comfortable with them before working on your hood.

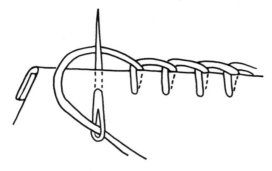

Figure B.7. This is the typical blanket stitch.
This diagram also shows the double-folded edge.

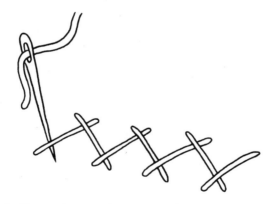

Figure B.8. This is the simple version of a herringbone stitch.

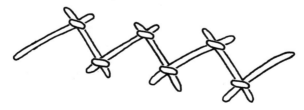

Figure B.9. In this stitch pattern, you can go back and cross the simple herringbone stitches you made in the previous stitch with a second color.

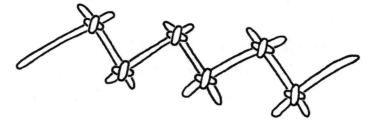

Figure B.10. Here is a more elaborate version of the herringbone with a second stitch that crossed over the first cross. While more time consuming, it makes a lovely decorative effect.

Figure B.11. The split stitch is great for "drawing" designs in thread or for other decorative effects. It is a backstitch where the needle is placed into the threads of the previous stitch.

APPENDIX C

Resources

ORGANIZATIONS

- **Author's website:** www.evelynrysdyk.com
- **Shaman Portal:** www.shamanportal.org
- **Shaman Links:** www.shamanlinks.net
- **The Society for Shamanic Practice:** www.shamansociety.org
- **Scandinavian Center for Shamanic Studies:** www.shamanism.dk
- **Circle of the Sacred Earth:** http://circleofthesacredearth.org
- **Shamanic Teachers and Practitioners:** www.shamanicteachers.com

PERIODICALS

- *Sacred Hoop* **Magazine:** www.sacredhoop.org

ATMOSPHERIC NORSE MUSIC

- *Norse Shaman-Seiðr Varðlokur*—**Spirit Passages:** A new recording to accompany seiðr that is especially useful for solo practitioners. It is sung in a minor key in keeping with Viking Age sensibilities. The recording also includes an opening galdr and closing galdr with callback signal. Available on iTunes and at www.spiritpassages .com/store.

- *Norse Oracle*—**Spirit Passages:** One-hour women's chorus to support a seiðr ritual that is especially useful for solo practitioners. Available on iTunes and at www.spiritpassages.com/store.
- *Wizard Women of the North*—**Various Artists:** Mesmerizing music by Scandinavian women musicians and singers that is out of print but available through Amazon.com. Listen to samples at www.allmusic.com/album/mw0000243305.
- *Gap Var Ginnunga* and *Yggdrasil*—**Wardruna:** Two CDs from a planned trilogy by a Norwegian group using ancient instruments and nature's rhythms to bring the energy of the runes to life. Available at www.wardruna.com.
- *Mahkalahke*—**Transjoik:** Haunting joik-inspired music by a Norwegian Sami male quartet. Available at www.transjoik.com.
- *Mannu*—**Angelit:** Contemporary Sami music by sisters Tuuni Partti and Ursula Länsman. This album is filled with marvelous and haunting vocals in the Sami language. Available at www.angelit.net.
- *The Stone Chair*—**Bukkene Bruse:** This Norwegian group consists of Arve Moen Bergset, Annbjørg Lien, Steinar Ofsdal, and Bjørn Ole Rasch; a cohesive ensemble of fiddles, flutes, voices, and electronic keyboards that has a slightly austere, almost medieval sound. Available at www.bjornolerasch.com/bukkenebruse.htm.

SHAMANIC SUPPLIES

- **Spirit Passages:** Drumming and meditation CDs, www.spiritpassages.com.
- **3Worlds:** Ritual objects for shamanic and Buddhist practice, www.3worlds.co.uk.
- **Shaman's Market:** South American shamanic practice items, www.shamansmarket.com.
- **Crazy Crow Trading:** Tools and supplies for shamanic crafting, www.crazycrow.com.

- **Mindfold:** Mask for journeying, www.mindfold.com.
- **Paine Products:** A source for balsam fir and cedar incense as well as bags of ground balsam fir, which is useful for making offerings in nature or to the fire, paineproducts.com.

VIKING-ERA JEWELRY AND CLOTHING RESOURCES

- **Urweg:** A jeweler in the USA making accurate, museum-quality replica brooches, necklaces, and pendants from the Viking and Anglo-Saxon periods, www.urweg.com.
- **Norðan:** A talented English jeweler, who lives and works in Germany making original, Viking Age jewelry, www.northan.net.
- **The Jelling Dragon:** This company in York, England, offers jewelry, clothing, and gear for Viking reenactors, www.jelldragon .com.
- **Wulflund:** Make your way through the convoluted website of this Czech pagan historical shop to discover jewelry, clothing, accessories, shoes, and crafting supplies fit for any Viking, www.wulflund .com. They also maintain an Etsy store.
- *Viking: Dress Clothing Garment* **by Nille Glaesel:** This is a wonderful book for those interested in making Viking-Era clothing for ritual wear. It is also illustrated with gorgeous photographs.

BOOKS FOR THE SHAMANIC JOURNEY PROCESS

- *Spirit Walking: A Course in Shamanic Power* by Evelyn C. Rysdyk
- *Shamanic Journeying: A Beginner's Guide* by Sandra Ingerman

Notes

INTRODUCTION.
THE POWER OF NORSE SHAMANISM

1. Stringer, "Modern Human Origins: Progress and Prospects," 563–79; Garrigan et al., "Evidence for Archaic Asian Ancestry on the Human X Chromosome," 189–92.

1. VISIONARIES IN OUR FAMILY TREE

1. Winkelman, "Shamans and Other 'Magico-Religious' Healers," 308–52.
2. Pearson, *Shamanism and the Ancient Mind,* 74.
3. Clottes, *The Shamans of Prehistory,* 12–19; John P. Miller, "Ancient Symbols in Rock Art," Bradford Foundation, www.bradshawfoundation .com/ancient_symbols_in_rock_art/index.php (accessed February 6, 2016).
4. Bourguignon, "Introduction: A Framework for the Comparative Study of Altered States of Consciousness," in *Religion, Altered States of Consciousness and Social Change,* 3–33.
5. Williams, *Prehistoric Belief,* 20.
6. Thomason, "The Role of Altered States of Consciousness in Native American Healing."
7. Williams, *Prehistoric Belief,* 20.
8. Harner and Tryon, "Psychological and Immunological Responses to Shamanic Journeying with Drumming."
9. Pringle, "New Women of the Ice Age."
10. Wright, "The Nature of the Shamanic State of Consciousness," 25–33.
11. Williams, *Prehistoric Belief,* 51.

12. Singh, "Shamans, Healing, and Mental Health," 131–34.

13. Rysdyk, *Spirit Walking: A Course in Shamanic Power,* 14–20.

14. Zvelebil, "Innovating Hunter-Gatherers," 18–59.

2. LONG AGO AND FAR AWAY: DISCOVERING OUR ANCESTORS' GIFTS

1. Fischer et al., "The Ancestor Effect," 11–16.

2. National Geographic Genographic Project, https://genographic.national geographic.com

3. Mathias et al., "Adaptive Evolution of the FADS Gene Cluster within Africa."

4. Hervella et al., "Ancient DNA from Hunter-Gatherer and Farmer Groups from Northern Spain Supports a Random Dispersion Model for the Neolithic Expansion into Europe."

5. University of Oxford, "Earliest Musical Instruments in Europe 40,000 Years Ago"; Universitaet Tübingen, "Oldest Art Even Older."

6. Washington University in St. Louis, "New Evidence for the Earliest Modern Humans in Europe."

7. Straus et al., eds, *Humans at the End of the Ice Age,* 146.

8. Czaplicka, *Aboriginal Siberia.* An online version of the 1914 edition has recently been made available at this address: https://archive.org/stream/aboriginalsiberi00czap#page/n1/mode/2up (accessed February 28, 2016); Straus et al., eds, *Humans at the End of the Ice Age,* 146.

9. National Oceanic and Atmospheric Administration, "The Younger Dryas," www.ncdc.noaa.gov/paleo/abrupt/data4.html (accessed February 28, 2016).

10. Plataforma SINC, "Farmers Slowed Down by Hunter-Gatherers."

11. Spinney, "Searching for Doggerland," 139.

12. Ibid., 143.

13. University College London, "Europe's First Farmers Were Immigrants."

14. University College Cork, "Origins of Farming in Europe Result of Human Migration and Cultural Change."

15. Bert Roberts, "Hobbits of Flores: Expert Q&A," Nova scienceNOW, April 1, 2005, www.pbs.org/wgbh/nova/evolution/little-people-flores-expert-q.html (accessed February 28, 2016).

16. Paterson, "Eskimo String Figures and Their Origin," 1–98.

17. Goucher et al., *In the Balance: Themes in World History*, selections from chapter 9 "Culture and Memory."

3. POWER IN THE FEMALE BODY

1. Tedlock, *The Woman in the Shaman's Body,* 28.
2. Caspari, "The Evolution of Grandparents."
3. Heather Pringle, "Ancient Sorcerer's 'Wake' Was First Feast for the Dead?" National Geographic Magazine, August 31, 2010, http://news .nationalgeographic.com/news/2010/08/100830-first-feast-science -proceedings-israel-shaman-sorcerer-tortoise/ (accessed February 28, 2016).
4. Hebrew University of Jerusalem, "Skeleton of 12,000-Year-Old Shaman Discovered Buried with Leopard, 50 Tortoises and Human Foot."
5. Hansen, "Archaeological Finds from Germany." (Booklet to the Photographic Exhibition.)
6. The Smithsonian National Museum of Natural History's Arctic Studies Center, www.mnh.si.edu/arctic/features/croads/ekven1.html#tomb (accessed February 28, 2016).
7. Czaplicka, *Aboriginal Siberia,* 243–56.
8. Vandiver et al., "The Origins of Ceramic Technology at Dolni Vestonice, Czechoslovakia," 1002–8.
9. Furholt et al., eds. "Megaliths and Identities. The Earliest Monuments in Europe," www.academia.edu/1346797/ (accessed February 28, 2016).
10. Dixson and Dixson, "Venus Figurines of the European Paleolithic."

5. THE FIRST SHAMAN BECOMES A GODDESS

1. Snorri Sturluson, "Ynglinga saga 4," in *Heimskringla, Volume 1,* translated by Alison Finlay and Anthony Faukes (London: Viking Society for Northern Research, 2011).

6. THE NORNS: MISTRESSES OF COSMIC PATTERNS

1. Bauschatz, *The Well and the Tree,* 3.
2. Jordi Estévez, "Catastrophes or Sudden Changes. The Need to Review Our Time Perspective in Prehistory," in *Vers une anthropologie des catastrophes Actes des 9e journées d'anthropologie de Valbonne,* edited by Luc Buchet, Catherine Rigeade, Isabelle Séguy, and Michel Signoli, Éditions APDCA-INED, Antibes, (2008): 22. www.academia.edu/876039 (accessed February 28, 2016).
3. Bauschatz, *The Well and the Tree,* 14.

4. Online Etymology Dictionary, http://etymonline.com (accessed February 28, 2016).

5. Gabriel Turville-Petre, *Origins of Icelandic Literature* (Oxford: Clarendon Press, 1953), 279.

6. Russell, "The Primacy of Consciousness."

7. Comings, "The New Physics of Space, Time and Light."

8. SEIÐR AS SHAMANIC RITUAL

1. Williams, "Oseberg Shamans: Sailing to Eternity."

2. Bjarnadóttir, *The Saga of Vanadis, Völva and Valkyrja*, 133.

3. Høst, "The Staff and the Song, Using the Old Norse Seidr in Modern Shamanism."

4. Dick Harrison and Kristina Svensson, *Vikingaliv* (Värnamo, Sweden: Fälth & Hässler, 2007), 57.

5. Wardwell, *Tangible Visions*, 218–33; Evelyn C. Rysdyk, *The Spirit Walker's Guide to Shamanic Tools* (San Francisco: Red Wheel/Weiser Books, 2014.)

6. Prokofyeva, "The Costume of an Enets Shaman," 154.

7. National Museum of Denmark, http://natmus.dk/en/historical-knowledge/denmark/prehistoric-period-until-1050-ad/the-viking-age/religion-magic-death-and-rituals/the-magic-wands-of-the-seeresses/ (accessed February 28, 2016).

8. Discussion of etymology of *seiðr*, www.princeton.edu/~achaney/tmve/wiki100k/docs/Seid.html.

9. Helgason et al., "Sequences from First Settlers Reveal Rapid Evolution in Icelandic mtDNA Pool."

10. Magnusson and Pálsson, trans., *The Vinland Sagas*, 81–84.

11. Bjarnadóttir and Kremer, "Prolegomena to a Cosmology of Healing in Vanir Norse Mythology," 163.

12. Näsström, *Freyja, the Great Goddess of the North*, 63.

13. John Martin Crawford, trans., "Proem," in *The Kalevala: Epic Poem of Finland*, 1888 (Penn State Electronic Classics Series Publication, 2004).

14. Blain, *Nine Worlds of Seid-Magic: Ecstasy and Neo-Shamanism in North European Paganism*, 62.

15. Bjarnadóttir and Kremer, "Prolegomena to a Cosmology of Healing in Vanir Norse Mythology," 164.

16. Gräslund, "Gamla Uppsala during the Migration Period," in *Myth, Might, and Man,* 11.

17. Naess, "Vikings' Afterlife Voyage."

18. Magnusson and Pálsson, trans., *The Vinland Sagas,* 81–84.

19. Czaplicka, *Aboriginal Siberia,* 203.

20. Gro Steinsland and P. Meulengracht Sørensen. *Människor och makter i vikingarnas värld* (Stockholm: Ordfront, 1998), 82.

21. Sigurd Grieg, *Osebergfundet,* vol. 2 (Oslo: Den Norsk Stat, 1928).

22. Price, "The Archaeology of Seiðr," 109–26.

23. Lissner, *Man, God and Magic,* 163.

24. Shepard and Sanders, *The Sacred Paw,* 60.

25. Gimbutas, *The Language of the Goddess,* 189.

26. Eldar Heide, "Spinning Seiðr," in *Old Norse Religion in Long-Term Perspectives: Origins, Changes and Interactions,* eds. Andres Andrén, Kristina Jennbert, and Catharina Raudvere (Lund, Sweden: Nordic Academic Press, 2006), 164–70.

27. Gardela, "Into Viking Minds," 64.

9. SEIÐR AND THE SAMI CONNECTION

1. Giuseppe Passarino, Gianpiero L. Cavalleri, Alice A. Lin, Luigi Luca Cavalli-Sforza, Anne-Lise Børresen-Dale, and Peter A. Underhill, "Different Genetic Components in the Norwegian Population Revealed by the Analysis of mtDNA and Y Chromosome Polymorphisms," *European Journal of Human Genetics* 10, no. 9 (2002): 521–29.

2. Pálsson, "The Sami People in Old Norse Literature," 29–33.

3. Price, *The Viking Way,* 237–38.

10. PREPARING TO PERFORM SEIÐR

1. Price, "The Archaeology of Seiðr," 109–26.

2. Bjarnadóttir and Kremer, "Prolegomena to a Cosmology of Healing in Vanir Norse Mythology," 163.

11. OTHER ACCOUTREMENTS OF THE VÖLVA

1. Price, *The Viking Way,* 171–73.

2. Ibid., 173.

12. ÚTISETA:
CONNECTING WITH NATURE'S POWER

1. L. Cruden, "Thoughts on Contemporary Vision Questing Practices," *Shaman's Drum*, Winter 1996, 19–22.
2. Marilyn Foster Riley and John C. Hendee, "Wilderness Vision Quest Clients: Motivations and Reported Benefits from an Urban-Based Program 1988 to 1997." Proceedings Rocky Mountain Research Station, USDA Forest Service (RMRS-P-14), 2000: 128–35. www.webpages.uidaho.edu/css491/readings/hendeevisionquest.PDF (accessed February 29, 2016).

14. THE MANY FACES OF SEIÐR

1. Price, *The Viking Way*, 227–32.

15. LEARNING TO SEE:
MEETING WITH ÓÐINN

1. Wells, *The Journey of Man*.
2. Martin Richards, "The Neolithic Invasion of Europe," *Annual Review Anthropology* 32 (2003): 135–62.
3. Diana L. Paxson, "Sex, Status, and Seidr: Homosexuality and Germanic Religion," www.seidh.org/articles/sex-status-seidh/ (accessed February 29, 2016).

16. THE NURTURING TREE

1. Judith Crews, "Forest and Tree Symbolism in Folklore," *Unasylva* 54, no. 213 (2003): 37–43.
2. Archaeologica.org Discussion Board, "In Search of the Palaeo Shaman," May 10, 2008, http://archaeologica.boardbot.com/viewtopic.php?f=12&t=1631 (accessed February 29, 2016).
3. Darl J. Dumont, "The Ash Tree in Indo-European Culture," *Mankind Quarterly* 32, no. 4 (1992): 323–36. www.musaios.com/ash.htm (accessed February 29, 2016).
4. Edwin Oliver James, *Tree of Life: An Archaeological Study* (Leiden, Netherlands: Brill, 1966), 163–64.
5. Christopher L.C.E. Witcomb, "Trees and the Sacred," Sacred Places, http://witcombe.sbc.edu/sacredplaces/trees.html (accessed February 29, 2016).
6. Anders Hultgård, "The Askr and Embla Myth in a Comparative Perspective."

7. Kristin G. Condon, *America Folk Art: A Regional Reference* (Santa Barbara, Calif.: ABC-CLIO, 2012), 47.

8. David Adams Leeming, *Creation Myths of the World: An Encyclopedia*, 2nd ed. (Santa Barbara, Calif.: ABC-CLIO, 2010), 307.

9. Benjamin Thorpe, trans., *The Elder Edda of Saemund Sigfusson* (London: Norrœna Society, 1907), 337.

10. James Owen, "Oldest Living Tree Found in Sweden," *National Geographic News,* April 14, 2008, http://news.nationalgeographic.com/news/2008/04/080414-oldest-tree.html (accessed February 29, 2016).

Glossary of Terms

Æsgard—The home of the Æsir deities.

Æsir—One of the families of deities of the Norse/Germanic people. The Vanir deities are the other family. The chief deity of the Æsir is Óðinn. He resides in Æsgard, a realm that lies at the top of the World Tree.

Ættir—A clan or family group.

Alfheim—The home of the light elves. These beings are like Celtic faeries and, like them, live in a betwixt and between realm just beyond/above the realm of humans.

Aurignacian—A term used to describe an Upper Paleolithic human culture that existed in Europe and southwestern Asia 45,000–35,000 years ago.

Austri—The dark elf/dwarf who holds up the eastern part of the sky. His companions Sudri, Vestri, and Nordi hold up the other corners of the sky. He and his brothers bestowed the necklace Brisingamen on Freyja in return for her sexual favors.

axis mundi—A central unifying principle that unites all of reality; it is the world center and the connection between the heavens, earth, and lower realms. It is sometimes represented as a great tree. (Also see World Tree.)

Bad Dürrenberg—A town in the Saalekreis district, in Saxony-Anhalt, Germany, where the remains of Neolithic female shaman were found.

bergrisi—A mountain jötunn, a mountain giant.

bergsrå—Female nature spirits who guard the mountains.

Brisingamen—The beautiful necklace of Freyja. The goddess slept with the dwarves or dark elves that hold up the sky to claim it as her own.

callback signal—The final rhythm in shamanic journey drumming that supports the journeyer to return to ordinary consciousness.

Chalcolithic—A word that refers to the Copper Age of human culture.

disir—Plural of *dis*. These are female protective deities. Disir include the lesser Norns, the fylgjur (animal protectors), and Valkyries who bring the slain in battle to their final rest. Their connection to the feminine gender implies that these concepts predate the arrival of Proto-Indo-European settlers to Europe. Norns are possibly a kind of disir or female protective deities as the word *dis* refers to the honorific term, *lady*.

Doggerland—A body of land that once connected the British Isles and Scandinavia to the European mainland. It was drowned as glaciers melted and two gigantic lakes of glacial melt water spilled their contents into the ocean around 8,200 years ago. The Storegga Slide of 6,100 BCE completed the inundation of Doggerland.

Dolni Věstonice—The Upper Paleolithic site in the Czech Republic where the remains of a 26,000-year-old female shaman were found. This shaman was also working and firing clay figures 15,000 years before pottery vessels were created elsewhere in the world.

Edda—The Icelandic Eddas are a body of long prose and poetic writings that tell of the ancient Icelanders.

effigy—A figurative representation of a spirit or living entity.

empower—The action of imbuing an object with the spiritual essence of a protective or healing entity.

Freyja—Goddess of the Vanir. She is the goddess of love, battle, healing, prophecy, magic, and beauty and receives half the valorous slain after battle.

Freyr—Brother to Freyja. He lives in and oversees Alfheim, the home of the light elves, which lies in the between place just above Midgard but below Æsgard.

fylgja—A Norse shaman's animal ally and spirit helper. Plural is fylgjur.

galdr—Refers to a spell, poetic incantation, or formal song with lyrics that can be used as an offering to the spirits, to raise power, to work magic, to inspire a community, or for other purpose. It can also be performed in combination with certain rites, such as in the seiðr ritual.

galdrakona—A woman who employed the use of incantations or chants; another name for the völva.

galdramaðr—A man who employed the use of incantations or chants.

gandr—A word that can mean spirit, ally, or magic, or all three at once.

gandreið—Riding a spirit or riding through the air by the use of an enchantment or spell.

gievre—A Sami frame drum that has a frame made from a bent slab of green wood.

goavdi—The unique bowl-shaped drum of the northern Sami people.

gyðja—A Norse priestess of sacrifices or offerings to the spirits. The goddess Freyja was said to be the first gyðja.

hamingja—The word means the personification of the good fortune or luck of an individual or family, as well as the altered appearance of a shapeshifter.

hamskipti—Shape-shifting; that is, taking on the shape or aspect of a spirit ally.

havsrå—Female nature spirits who protect saltwater.

Hildisvíni—The boar that Freyja rides into battle.

huldre/huldra—Female forest spirits, who appear as beautiful women in the front and have animal tails and either hollow or bark-covered backs.

husvaettir—The spirits that protect the home and hearth.

jhankri—A Nepalese shaman.

jötunn—Giant in Old Norse. The jötunn were primordial beings and predecessors of the gods. They reside in Jötunnheim, a realm to the east of Midgard.

Juksáhkká—The Sami goddess known as "Bow Woman" or "Bow Mother" who can make an unborn child male and instructs boys. She lives at the hearth of the home. Daughter of Máttaráhkká.

landvættir—Nature spirits that enliven and protect the landscape.

lavuu—The conical tent used by traditional, nomadic Sami reindeer herders.

matricentric—Centered around the female or mother.

Máttaráhkká—The Sami people's Great Mother Goddess, who has three daughters: Sáráhkká, Juksáhkká, and Uksáhkká.

Midgard—The ancient Norse spirit realm that contains the human world.

noaide—The Sami term for shaman.

Nordi—The dark elf/dwarf who holds up the northern part of the sky. His companions Austri, Vestri, and Sudri hold up the other corners of the sky. He and his brothers bestowed the necklace Brisingamen on Freyja in return for her sexual favors.

Norns—In Norse mythology the Norns are female jötunn (giants) who rule over the destiny of gods and men. While there are many lesser Norns, the primary Norns are the three sisters Urð (Wyrd), Verðandi, and Skuld who reside at the base of the World Tree, Yggdrasil. They support and nurture Yggdrasil, as well as create and work the threads of time and matter.

Óðinn—Also known as Odin. Óðinn is the chief of the Æsir family of Norse/Germanic deities.

ogham—An early Medieval Celtic magical alphabet in which each letter correlates to a different species of tree.

oova—A Tuvan term for sacred cairn, large stone, or post erected on the landscape that is then used as a receptacle for offerings.

oovo—A Mongolian term for a sacred cairn, large stone, or post erected on the landscape that is used as a receptacle for offerings.

Ørlög—The patterns of cosmic space, time, and fate. The Norse concept of Ørlög has been described as a primordial law or template for reality—

what I think of as the quantum plenum or playing field of infinite possibilities. The fabric of energy or light from which all matter is born.

power animal—A protective spirit of a shaman or Spirit walker that may be accessed for guidance or merged with for personal protection or to "borrow" the animal's senses for the purpose of healing or divination. (Also see fylgja.)

Ráddiolmmái—The Sami supreme deity who is a silent and impartial ruler. Humans sought to influence other gods who were personifications of natural forces because of Ráddiolmmái's distance from the daily affairs of the human or natural world.

raddlið—The small chorus of women who sing the varðlokur songs for the seiðr ritual.

runes—A Northern European (Norse/Germanic) magical alphabet that predates the use of the Latin alphabet and may still be used for divination.

saiven—The Ulchi word for a spirit effigy that is usually made from wood.

šaman—Tungus-Mongol language term for shaman.

Sami—The indigenous people of Arctic Scandinavia and the Kola Peninsula. Their traditional homeland known as Sápmi ranges across the countries of Norway, Sweden, Finland, and Russia.

Sáráhkká—The Sami goddess that creates and molds the unborn baby's body around the soul. She is also invoked for easing childbirth. Her name translates to "opening or cleaving" "woman, wife, or mother." Daughter of Máttaráhkká.

scrying—The art of seeing the spirits in or performing divination with a shiny/opaque surface.

seiðhjallr—The ritual seat on which the völva sits for the seiðr ritual.

seiðkona—A woman who prophesies; another term for the völva.

seiðmaðr—A man who practices; a seiðr-man; a man who prophecies.

seiðr—A Norse divination ritual performed by women, and rarely by men, that involves a journey into the world of the deceased ancestors to receive guidance. It is performed by the völva, whose shamanic journey is accompanied by a women's chorus.

seiðstafr—Also known as a völ. The staff used in the seiðr ritual.

shaman—A person who by shifting consciousness enters the spirit world to communicate with the spirits for the purpose of healing, divination, guidance, and insight. This term is usually used to designate a person with a tribal affiliation.

shamanic journey—The altered-consciousness experience of a shaman or spirit walker that allows the practitioner to interact with the enlivening essences of nature and other beings that populate the spirit realms.

shamanic state of consciousness—The state of being attained by a shaman or spirit walker while journeying that allows them to experience the normally invisible worlds of spirit. This state may be attained through a repetitive stimulus such as drumming or rattling, chanting or dancing, as well as through the use of entheogenic compounds.

sjörå—Female nature spirits who protect lakes.

smudge—Ritual of fumigating with an herbal smoke for healing, clearing, or blessing a person or place.

spákona—A female Norse woman seer who, while in a shamanic trance, enters the roots of the great World Tree, Yggdrasil, to gain access to ancestral wisdom. The ritual in which this prophecy is received is known as seiðr. Also referred to as a völva or seiðkona.

spirit walker—A person called to the shamanic path who has developed a deep relationship with the spirits in the manner of a powerful tribal shaman. They may also be called to fill the role of shaman healer or diviner.

Storegga Slide—An underwater landslide off the coast of Norway in 6,100 BCE that created an enormous tsunami that drowned the last of Doggerland and cut the channel that separates England from France.

Sudri—The dark elf/dwarf who holds up the southern part of the sky. His companions Austri, Vestri, and Nordi hold up the other corners of the sky. He and his brothers bestowed the necklace Brisingamen on Freyja in return for her sexual favors.

svartálfar—A dark elf or dwarf.

Swartailfheim—Home of the dark elves or dwarves of Norse/Germanic mythology. This realm lies just beyond/beneath Midgard and is a between realm like the home of the light elves, Alfheim.

taufr—Old Norse word for magic and also for talismans, charms, and ritual objects. It is related to the Anglo-Saxon word for red ochre, a pigment used for magical purposes as early as the Neanderthal period in Europe. Ancient shaman bodies in Eurasia were heavily painted with red ochre prior to burial.

thermohaline circulation—The planet wide current of water that flows throughout the Earth's oceans.

tupilak—An Inuit term for spirit figures that looked like monsters made from different parts of people and animals. When used for malevolent purposes, images like these could be used to control an evil or disease-causing spirit for the purpose of causing harm.

tutelary spirits—The benevolent spirits with which a spirit walker or shaman communicates.

Uksáhkká—The Sami goddess known as "Door Wife," "Door Woman," or "Door Mother." She lives at the entrance of the home and offers protection against all evil entering the home. Daughter of Máttaráhkká.

Ulchi—A people from the Lower Amur River Basin of Siberia's far east who are part of the Tungusic language group. The Ulchi refer to themselves as Nani, though that name was applied to a neighboring people by the Russians in the 1930s.

Urð—Also Urðr. Eldest of the three Norns who reside at the base of the World Tree, Yggdrasil. Her sisters are Verðandi, who is younger, and Skuld, the youngest.

Urðarbrunnr—Urð's magical well, spring, or freshwater sea at the base of the World Tree, Yggdrasil. Also known as the well of remembrance. The twelfth-century Icelandic writer Snorri Sturluson suggested the existence of three wells. These are Urðarbrunnr, Hveergelmir (which means "bubbling, boiling spring" in Old Norse), and Mímisbrunnr (the well of the giant Mimir, "the rememberer" or "wise one"). This peculiar circumstance is most likely an error in Snorri's understanding of the old stories. It is more likely that there is only one source and that it is the well of memory, of wisdom, and the ultimate sacred creative vessel.

útiseta—A "sitting out," a ritual to seek a vision or commune with the spirits.

Vanaheim—Home of the Vanir deities, which lies to the west of Midgard.

Vanir—One of the two families of Norse/Germanic deities. The most prominent deity of this family is the goddess Freyja. The Æsir gods and goddesses are the other family of deities.

varðlokur—The spirit-calling chants or songs used in seiðr rituals—these differ from galdr as they are not poetic incantations, formal songs with lyrics used for offerings, or "spells" but rather repetitive songs to induce or maintain trance, to awaken ritual objects, and for other shamanic uses.

Verðandi—One of the three Norns who reside at the base of the World Tree, Yggdrasil. Of her sisters, Urð is oldest and Skuld the youngest.

Vestri—The dark elf/dwarf who holds up the western part of the sky. His companions Austri, Sudri, and Nordi hold up the other corners of the sky. He and his brothers bestowed the necklace Brisingamen on Freyja in return for her sexual favors.

vitki—A male sorcerer.

völ—The staff used in seiðr rituals. Also called a seiðstafr.

Völuspá—The Icelandic prose poem describing the work of the völva.

völva—(plural: völur) A female Norse woman seer who, while in a shamanic trance, enters the roots of the great World Tree, Yggdrasil, to gain access to ancestral wisdom. The ritual in which this prophecy is received is known as seiðr. Also referred to as a spákona.

World Tree—A uniting principle that connects the shamanic realms of the Upper, Middle, and Lower Worlds represented as an enormous tree, that which holds all of reality.

Wyrd—Another name for the Norn Urð. The manifesting of the path, the unfolding of fate, the action of manifesting physical matter. How consciousness "crystalizes" light into matter.

Yggdrasil—The Norse name for the World Tree. Yggdrasil is the uniting principle that connects all of the nine realms of the Norse/Germanic spirit world and that holds all spirit and matter.

yirka-laul-vairgin—Chukchee expression that means "soft man" and refers to the male shaman whose costume resembles women's clothing.

Bibliography

Adovasio, J. M., Olga Soffer, and Jake Page. *The Invisible Sex: Uncovering the True Roles of Women in Prehistory*. Walnut Creek, Calif.: Left Coast Press, 2007.

Bauschatz, Paul C. *The Well and the Tree: World and Time in Early Germanic Culture*. Amherst: University of Massachusetts Press, 1982.

Bellows, Henry Adams, trans. *The Poetic Edda*. Princeton, N.J.: Princeton University Press, 1936. www.sacred-texts.com.

Bjarnadóttir, Valgerður Hjördís. *The Saga of Vanadis, Völva and Valkyrja*. Saarbrücken, Germany: Lambert Academic Publishing, 2009. www.scribd .com/doc/103315274

Bjarnadóttir, Valgerður H., and Jürgen W. Kremer. "Prolegomena to a Cosmology of Healing in Vanir Norse Mythology." *Yearbook of Cross-Cultural Medicine and Psychology,* 1998/99: 125–74.

Blain, Jenny. *Nine Worlds of Seid-Magic: Ecstasy and Neo-Shamanism in North European Paganism*. London: Routledge, 2001.

Bourguignon, Erika. "Introduction: A Framework for the Comparative Study of Altered States of Consciousness." In *Religion, Altered States of Consciousness and Social Change,* edited by Erika Bourguignon. Columbus: Ohio State University, 1973.

Brink, Stefan, ed. *The Viking World*. In collaboration with Neil Price. London: Routledge, 2012.

Caspari, Rachel. "The Evolution of Grandparents." *Scientific American* 305, no. 2 (August 2011): 44–49. www.scientificamerican.com/article .cfm?id=the-evolution-of-grandparents.

Clottes, Jean. *The Shamans of Prehistory*. New York: Harry N. Abrams Publishers, 1998.

Comings, Mark. *The New Physics of Space, Time and Light*. Keynote address, True North Annual Conference, Portland, Maine, 2005. (The recording of the address is no longer available.)

Czaplicka, M. A. *Aboriginal Siberia: A Study in Social Anthropology*. 1914. Reprint, London: Oxford University Press, 1969.

Devlet, Ekaterina. "Rock Art and the Material Culture of Siberian and Central Asian Shamanism." Chap. 3 in *The Archaeology of Shamanism*, edited by Neil Price. New York: Routledge, 2001.

Dixson, Alan F., and Barnaby J. Dixson. "Venus Figurines of the European Paleolithic: Symbols of Fertility or Attractiveness?" *Journal of Anthropology*, 2011, Article ID 569120. http://dx.doi.org/10.1155/2011/569120.

Dyrenkova, N. P. "Bear Worship among Turkish Tribes of Siberia," Proceedings of the 23rd International Congress of Americanists (1928), 411–44. New York, 1930.

Eliade, Mircea. *Shamanism: Archaic Techniques of Ecstasy*. Princeton, N.J.: Princeton University Press, 1964.

Fedorova, Natalia. "Shamans, Heroes and Ancestors Bronze Castings of Western Siberia." Chap. 4 in *The Archaeology of Shamanism*, edited by Neil Price. New York: Routledge, 2001.

Fischer, P., A. Sauer, C. Vogrincic, and S. Weisweiler. "The Ancestor Effect: Thinking about our Genetic Origin Enhances Intellectual Performance." *European Journal of Social Psychology* 41, no. 1 (2010): 11–16.

Furholt, Martin, Friedrich Lüth, and Johannes Müller, eds. "Megaliths and Identities. The Earliest Monuments in Europe: Architecture and Social Structures (5000–3000 BC)." In *Journal from the 3rd European Megalithic Studies Group Meeting* (May 2010), 15–32. Bonn, Germany: Dr. Rudolf Habelt, 2011.

Gardela, Leszek. "Into Viking Minds: Reinterpreting the Staffs of Sorcery and Unraveling Seiðr." In *Viking and Medieval Scandinavia*, vol. 4. Turnhout, Belgium: Brepols Publishers, 2008.

Garrigan, D., Z. Mobasher, T. Severson, J .A. Wilder, and M. F. Hammer. "Evidence for Archaic Asian Ancestry on the Human X Chromosome." *Molecular Biology and Evolution* 22, no. 2 (2005): 189–92.

Gimbutas, Marija. *The Language of the Goddess*. San Francisco: Harper, 1989.

Glaesel, Nille. *Viking: Dress, Garment, Clothing.* 2nd ed. Printed by CreateSpace, 2014.

Goucher, Candice, Charles LeGuin, and Linda Walton. "Culture and Memory." Chap. 9 in *In the Balance: Themes in World History.* Boston: McGraw-Hill, 1998.

Gräslund, B. "Gamla Uppsala during the Migration Period." In *Myth, Might, and Man.* Stockholm: Swedish National Heritage Board, 2000.

Hagens, Bethe. "Venuses, Turtles and Other Hand-held Cosmic Models." In *On Semiotic Modeling,* edited by Myrdene Anderson and Floyd Merrell, 47–60. Berlin: Mouton de Guyter, 1991.

Hansen, Svend. "Archaeological Finds from Germany." (Booklet to the Photographic Exhibition) Institutum Archaeologicum Germanicum, 2010. (This is no longer available.)

Harner, Sandra, and Warren W. Tryon. "Psychological and Immunological Responses to Shamanic Journeying with Drumming." *Shaman* 4, nos. 1–2 (1996): 89–97.

Hebrew University of Jerusalem. "Skeleton of 12,000-Year-Old Shaman Discovered Buried with Leopard, 50 Tortoises and Human Foot." *ScienceDaily*, November 5, 2008. www.sciencedaily.com/releases/2008/11/081105083721.htm (accesssed February 27, 2016).

Helgason. A., C. Lalueza-Fox, S. Ghosh, S. Sigurðardóttir, M. L. Sampietro et al. "Sequences from First Settlers Reveal Rapid Evolution in Icelandic mtDNA Pool." *PLoS Genet* 5, no. 1 (2009). http://journals.plos.org/plos-genetics/article?id=10.1371/journal.pgen.1000343 (accessed February 27, 2016).

Hervella, M., N. Izagirre, S. Alonso, R. Fregel, A. Alonso et al. "Ancient DNA from Hunter-Gatherer and Farmer Groups from Northern Spain Supports a Random Dispersion Model for the Neolithic Expansion into Europe." *PLoS ONE* 7, no. 4 (2012). http://journals.plos.org/plosone/article?id=10.1371/journal.pone.0034417 (accessed February 27, 2016).

Holmes, Hannah. *Suburban Safari: A Year on the Lawn.* New York: Bloomsbury Publishing, 2005.

Høst, Annette. "The Staff and the Song, Using the Old Norse Seidr in Modern Shamanism." www.shamanism.dk/seidrstaffsong.htm (accessed February 27, 2016).

Hultgård, Anders. "The Askr and Embla Myth in a Comparative Perspective."

Old Norse Religion in Long-Term perspectives: Origins, Changes and Interactions. Andrén, Andres, Kristina Jennbert, and Catharina Raudvere, eds. Lund, Sweden: Nordic Academic Press, 2006.

Ingerman, Sandra. *The Beginner's Guide to Shamanic Journeying.* Louisville, Colo.: Sounds True, 2008.

Janhunen, Juha. "Tracing the Bear Myth in Northeast Asia." *Acta Slavica Iaponica* 20 (2003): 1–24. An English language version of this article can be found online at: http://src-home.slav.hokudai.ac.jp/publictn/acta/20/asi20-001-janhunen.pdf (accessed February 27, 2016).

Kelly, Karen. "Thorbjorg's Story, An Introduction to Seiðr." *Spirit Talk* 9 (Early Summer 1999).

Lindow, John. *Norse Mythology: A Guide to the Gods, Heroes, Rituals, and Beliefs.* Oxford: Oxford University Press, 2001.

Lissner, Ivar. *Man, God and Magic.* New York: Putnam, 1961.

Louis, Roberta. "Shamanic Healing Practices of the Ulchi." *Shaman's Drum Magazine,* no. 53 (Fall 1999): 51–60.

Magnusson, Magnus, and Hermann Pálsson, trans. *The Vinland Sagas.* London: Penguin, 1965.

Mathias, Rasika A., Wenqing Fu, Joshua M. Akey, Hannah C. Ainsworth, Dara G. Torgerson, Ingo Ruczinski, Susan Sergeant, Kathleen C. Barnes, Floyd H. Chilton. "Adaptive Evolution of the FADS Gene Cluster within Africa." *PLoS ONE* 7, no. 9 (2012). http://journals.plos.org/plosone/article?id=10.1371/journal.pone.0044926 (accessed February 28, 2016).

Metzner, Ralph. *The Well of Remembrance: Rediscovering the Earth Wisdom Myths of Northern Europe.* Boston, Mass.: Shambhala, 1994.

Mundal, Else. "The Perception of the Saamis and Their Religion in Old Norse Sources." In *Shamanism and Northern Ecology,* edited by Juha Pentikäinen, 97–116. New York: Mouton de Gruyter, 1996.

Muus, Nathan. "The Sami Drum." *Baiki, The North American Sami Journal* 17 (Winter 1998).

Naess, Ellen Marie. "Vikings' Afterlife Voyage." *Current World Archeology,* no. 45 (2011): 48–52.

Näsström, Britt-Mari. *Freyja, the Great Goddess of the North.* Lund, Sweden: University of Lund, 1995.

Pálsson, Hermann. "The Sami People in Old Norse Literature." *Nordlit: Tidsskrift i litteratur og kultur* 5 (1999): 29–53. An English version of this article can be found at septentrio.vit.no/index.php/nordlit/article/ view/2143/2000 (accessed February 28, 2016).

Paterson, T. T. "Eskimo String Figures and Their Origin." *Acta Arctica* 3 (1949): 1–98.

Pearson, James L. *Shamanism and the Ancient Mind: A Cognitive Approach to Archaeology.* Walnut Creek, Calif.: Altamira Press, 2002.

Plataforma SINC. "Farmers Slowed Down by Hunter-Gatherers: Our Ancestors' Fight for Space." *ScienceDaily,* December 3, 2010. www .sciencedaily.com/releases/2010/12/101203081642.htm (accessed February 28, 2016).

Price, Neil S. "The Archaeology of Seiðr: Circumpolar Traditions in Viking Pre-Christian Religion." *Brathair* 4, no. 2 (2004): 109–126. http://ppg.revistas .uema.br/index.php/brathair/article/view/616 (accessed February 28, 2016).

Price, Neil S. *The Viking Way: Religion and War in Late Iron Age Scandinavia.* Uppsala, Sweden: Uppsala University, 2002.

Price, Neil S. "Wooden Worlds: Individual and Collective in the Chamber Graves of Birka." In *Birka Nu: Pågående Forskning Om Världsarvet Birka Och Hovgården,* edited by Charlotte Hedenstierna-Jonson, 81–94. Stockholm: Historika Museet, 2012.

Pringle, Heather. "New Women of the Ice Age." *Discover Magazine* 19, no. 4, April 1998.

Prokofyeva, Ye. D. "The Costume of an Enets Shaman." In *Studies in Siberian Shamanism,* edited by Henry N. Michael. Toronto: University of Toronto Press for the Arctic Institute of North America, 1963.

Russell, Peter. "The Primacy of Consciousness." www.peterrussell.com/SP/ PrimConsc.php

Rysdyk, Evelyn C. *Spirit Walking: A Course in Shamanic Power.* San Francisco: RedWheel/Weiser, Inc., 2013.

Serov, S. Ia. "Guardians and Spirit-masters of Siberia." In *Crossroads of Continents,* edited by W. W Fitzhugh and A. Crowell, 247–49. Washington, DC: Smithsonian Institution, 1988.

Shepard, Paul, and Barry Sanders. *The Sacred Paw: The Bear in Nature, Myth and Literature.* New York: Viking Penguin, Inc., 1985.

Singh, Ashvind N. "Shamans, Healing, and Mental Health." *Journal of Child and Family Studies* 8, no. 2 (1999): 131–34.

Spinney, Laura. "Searching for Doggerland." *National Geographic Magazine* 222, no. 6, December 2012.

Straus, Lawrence Guy, Berit Valentin Eriksen, Jon M. Erlandson, and David R. Yester, eds. *Humans at the End of the Ice Age: The Archaeology of the Pleistocene-Holocene Transition*. New York: Plenum Press, 1996.

Stringer, Chris, "Modern Human Origins: Progress and Prospects." *Philosophical Transactions of the Royal Society of London* 357, no. 1420 (2002): 563–79. www.ncbi.nlm.nih.gov/pmc/articles/PMC1692961/pdf/12028792.pdf (accessed February 28, 2016).

Talbot, Michael. *The Holographic Universe*. New York: HarperCollins Publishers, 1992.

Tedlock, Barbara. *The Woman in the Shaman's Body*. New York: Bantam/Dell, 2005.

Thomason, Timothy C. "The Role of Altered States of Consciousness in Native American Healing." *Journal of Rural Community Psychology* E13, no. 1 (2010). www.marshall.edu/jrcp/VE13%20N1/jrcp%2013%201%20thomason .pdf (accessed February 28, 2016).

Universitaet Tübingen. "Oldest Art Even Older: New Dates from Geißenklösterle Cave Show Early Arrival of Modern Humans, Art and Music." *ScienceDaily*, May 24, 2012. www.sciencedaily.com/releases/2012/05/120524092226 .htm (accessed February 28, 2016).

University College Cork. "Origins of Farming in Europe Result of Human Migration and Cultural Change, Study Suggests." *ScienceDaily*, February 22, 2011. www.sciencedaily.com/releases/2011/02/110222192828.htm (accessed February 28, 2016).

University College London. "Europe's First Farmers Were Immigrants: Replaced Their Stone Age Hunter-gatherer Forerunners." *ScienceDaily*, September 4, 2009. www.sciencedaily.com/releases/2009/09/090903163902.htm (accessed February 28, 2016).

University of Arizona. "Ancient Humans Were Mixing It Up: Anatomically Modern Humans Interbred with More Archaic Hominin Forms while in Africa." *ScienceDaily*, September 6, 2011. www.sciencedaily.com/ releases/2011/09/110905160918.htm (accessed February 28, 2016).

University of Oxford. "Earliest Musical Instruments in Europe 40,000 Years Ago." *ScienceDaily*, May 27, 2012. www.sciencedaily.com/releases/ 2012/05/120527195720.htm (accessed February 28, 2016).

Vandiver, P., O. Soffer, B. Klima, and J. Svoboda. "The Origins of Ceramic

Technology at Dolni Vestonice, Czechoslovakia." *Science* 246, no. 4933 (1989): 1002–8.

Vitebsky, Piers. *The Shaman*. Boston: Little Brown and Company, 1995.

Wardwell, Allen. *Tangible Visions*. New York: Monacelli Press, 1996.

Washington University in St. Louis. "New Evidence for the Earliest Modern Humans in Europe." *ScienceDaily,* November 2, 2011. www.sciencedaily .com/releases/2011/11/111102161141.htm (accessed February 28, 2016).

Wells, Spencer. *The Journey of Man: A Genetic Odyssey*. Princeton, N.J.: Princeton University Press, 2002.

Williams, Mike. "Oseberg Shamans: Sailing to Eternity." *Prehistoric Shamanism Blog,* March 25, 2011. (Blog entry is no longer available online.)

Williams, Mike. *Prehistoric Belief.* Gloucestershire, UK: The History Press, 2011.

Winkelman, Michael. "Shamans and Other 'Magico-Religious' Healers: A Cross-Cultural Study of Their Origins, Nature, and Social Transformations." *Ethos* 18, no. 3 (1990): 308–52. www.jstor.org/stable/640339 (accessed February 28, 2016).

Winkelman, Michael. "Trance States: A Theoretical Model and Cross-Cultural Analysis." *Ethos* 14, no. 2 (1986): 174–203. www.jstor.org/stable/639951 (accessed February 28, 2016).

Wright, P. A. "The Nature of the Shamanic State of Consciousness: A Review." *Journal of Psychoactive Drugs* 21, no. 1 (1989): 25–33.

Zvelebil, Marek. "Innovating Hunter-Gatherers: The Mesolithic in the Baltic." Chap. 2 in *Mezolithic Europe,* edited by Geoff Bailey and Penny Spikins. Cambridge: Cambridge University Press, 2010.

Index

About the Author

Nationally recognized shaman teacher/healer, speaker, and author of *Spirit Walking: A Course in Shamanic Power, A Spirit Walker's Guide to Shamanic Tools,* and *Modern Shamanic Living: New Explorations of an Ancient Path* and contributor to *Spirited Medicine: Shamanism in Contemporary Healthcare,* Evelyn C. Rysdyk delights in supporting people to remember their sacred place in All That Is. Whether through face-to-face contact with individual patients, workshop groups and conference participants, or through the printed word, Evelyn uses her loving humor and passion to open people's hearts and inspire them to live more joyful, fulfilling, and purposeful lives. Her website is

www.evelynrysdyk.com.

Evelyn praying to the ancestors on the northern coast of Iceland.

BOOKS OF RELATED INTEREST

Icelandic Magic
Practical Secrets of the Northern Grimoires
by Stephen Flowers

Pagan Magic of the Northern Tradition
Customs, Rites, and Ceremonies
by Nigel Pennick

Siberian Shamanism
The Shanar Ritual of the Buryats
by Virlana Tkacz
with Sayan Zhambalov and Wanda Phipps
Photographs by Alexander Khantaev

Speaking with Nature
Awakening to the Deep Wisdom of the Earth
by Sandra Ingerman and Llyn Roberts

Secret Medicines from Your Garden
Plants for Healing, Spirituality, and Magic
by Ellen Evert Hopman

A Druid's Herbal for the Sacred Earth Year
by Ellen Evert Hopman

The Gift of Shamanism
Visionary Power, Ayahuasca Dreams, and Journeys to Other Realms
by Itzhak Beery
Foreword by John Perkins

Shamanic Breathwork
Journeying beyond the Limits of the Self
by Linda Star Wolf

INNER TRADITIONS • BEAR & COMPANY
P.O. Box 388 • Rochester, VT 05767
1-800-246-8648 • www.InnerTraditions.com

Or contact your local bookseller